Not Normal

The uncensored account of an
extraordinary true-life story

Paul Connolly

Not Normal

ISBN : 9781982908713

This edition published 2019

by Paul Connolly Ltd

All rights reserved.

To learn more:

facebook.com/notnormalbook

Paulconnolly.com

Specialistconditioning.com

I have described events, locales and conversations from my memories. In order to maintain anonymity in some instances I have changed the names of individuals, places or identifying characteristics and details such as physical properties, occupations and places of residence.

Acknowledgements

The question I am asked most often - "How did you survive, when so many of your friends did not?". Simple answer, the love of people, the loving connection of people.

Mary Cuckney, my nurse in St Vincent's Children's Home, who loved me when at two weeks old, I was given to this young 18 year old nurse to look after. We still talk today and I owe her my life.

Alan, my boxing coach and his wife Cathy, without whom my daily beating by Bill Starling would have continued for many more years and I may have not have lived on much longer, I owe them my life too.

Liam Carroll, my best friend from St Leonards Children's Home who looked after me when we were targeted at school for being kids in care, I loved Liam so much and miss him every day. RIP my brother.

Ian Mecklenburgh, my friend of 30 years, has put up with my crazy forever and will definitely go to heaven. Ian has always been there for me, even when he was way out of his comfort zone. Thank you does not really cover it mate.

Richard Hart, responsible for my story hitting the big screen. Richard gets shit done, like no one I have ever met before!

Boo, Jo Cole. My wife, the mother of my two amazing sons - Harley and Archie. The woman who taught me right from wrong, who has stood by me for 16 years with the emotional strength that only a saint could muster, any normal woman would have left me years ago.

There are many other good friends that have had my back over the years, too many to mention, they know who they are and that I am here for them as well.

Thank you everyone for making that connection with love, the most powerful energy. Building self-esteem and real belief in our children is far easier than mending broken adults... What happens to us as children, will determine the rest of our lives. We have a responsibility to our children and the future of mankind....

V

Foreword

Most people don't like reading about child abuse. Why would they? Learning how kids have been raped and horribly neglected is the stuff of nightmares. Others struggle to believe such abuse can even happen in the UK, the fifth richest nation.

Yet it does. And not believing kids is one reason why abusers get away with it.

Six out of eight of the boys I shared my dormitory with at St Leonard's, a children's home run by child abusers between 1970 and 1982, are dead – some by suicide, others by drug addiction, but all of us lost our lives the day we arrived. How can kids who experienced such horrors grow up to be normal, happy adults? Well, they can't. The mental and physical torture I survived has stayed with me. All day, every day, it's always there in the background.

Forty years later, the fight for justice goes on. I've told my story before, but I never got to tell everything. Partly because, as a survivor of abuse, I'd buried a lot of what happened, and partly because some of the facts were deemed too shocking or obscene to tell. But now is the time to reveal everything.

In 2014, an independent inquiry into child abuse was opened and St Leonard's Children's Home in Hornchurch is one of many care homes being looked into. It's a long, complicated process and investigations reach as high as MPs in Westminster. But even this investigation has been full of controversy, and last year the Survivors of Organised and Institutional Abuse withdrew from the inquiry, calling it 'not fit for purpose'.

But whatever this ongoing inquiry is hoping to achieve, it's all too little, too late. Many kids who were abused in care don't live long, healthy lives. Their memories are like a nightmare they can't wake from and adulthood becomes unbearable.

When I was a kid, my carers tried to bugger me, they beat me and they verbally abused me, yet I count myself as one of the lucky ones. Despite everything, I survived to have a good career, get married and have kids of my own. So I've spent the last ten years speaking up for all those who didn't.

St Leonard's was set up to be an idyllic home where abandoned kids would be cared for. But instead it became a private kingdom where paedophiles were kings and child abusers were queens. Hundreds of staff worked with over three-thousand children from 1965 to 1984, and yet to date only two have been caught and sentenced for abuse. In 2001, Bill Starling was found guilty of indecently assaulting, raping or buggering eleven victims – aged from just five to fourteen – over a twenty-year period. Alan Prescott, who was not only a local magistrate and GP but also a former social services director, had indecently assaulted four teenage boys between 1970 and 1980. He was a man who served in very powerful positions. Unbelievably, even *after* being convicted, Prescott was re-employed by the same council (Tower Hamlets) who ran St Leonard's.

Then of course there was Haydn Davies. An ex-army man, he was originally up for thirty-seven charges of indecent assault, but they had to drop the cases as the police, who cocked up the whole investigation, lost vital evidence. Davies is a man who was convicted in 1981 for buggering a teenage boy and yet was allowed to return to work with, yep, teenage boys.

You couldn't make this stuff up. Worse still, video evidence for the cases against both Prescott and Davies somehow got lost. This led to charges being dropped.

I believe that what went on at St Leonard's is just the tip of the iceberg when it comes to a network of child abuse. As recently as 2014, a Freedom of Information Act request asking for all the files relating to our home was denied by Tower Hamlets Council. Why was this? What have they got to hide? Also, why has nobody investigated how the police lost vital evidence during the 2001 case?

Even today more cases are coming out of the woodwork. In 2017, Paul Setchfield was jailed for nine years for eleven counts of indecently assaulting a young girl and boy, both aged under fourteen, at St Leonard's. He'd take them off to sleep in his private quarters; a practice I knew went on when I was there.

On a positive note, we have to look to the future and our duty to make sure this can never happen again. I am a core participant in the Historical Child Abuse enquiry set up by the UK government, this enquiry was set up by Theresa May while Home Secretary to learn from the lessons of the past. There are lots of good people out there in positions of power, I found this out with my work with Lord Listowell (Francis to me) and charities like Kids Inspire, Beanstalk and the NSPCC. But sadly, good people doing good things doesn't make the news.

With my movie coming out, and with this, my third book, I am hoping to raise my profile high enough to shame the powers that be into understanding that the desperate lack of investment in our kids over the last few decades is now proving to be devastating.

I've had to change some names for legal reasons – 'Auntie Coral' isn't her real name (police couldn't charge her for mental torture) – but aside from small changes, this is a true, uncensored account, including details never told before.

Paul Connolly, March, 2018

Contents:

Prologue

In my dormitory bed, wearing those old-fashioned stripy pyjamas, I feel my heart racing.

They're coming! A child's voice screams, and I don't know if it's mine. I'm scrambling for the kitchen knife hidden under my pillow. Got it! I clutch its wooden handle, comforted for moments, before the screaming gets louder. We know what's coming. We know what to expect. But there's no escape.

I jump onto my mattress, swinging my knife to and fro. For a split second everyone falls still as thirty pairs of eyes turn to the window. And then the shadows appear.

They're here!

I see men running up the fire escape, one by one. Our house 'parent', Uncle Bill, leads, followed by others with faces covered with black balaclava masks. Kids as young as four and five scatter like mice — under beds, under blankets, huddled in corners. Everyone is trying to hide, but there is nowhere to hide.

Quick, run! But there is nowhere to run before the door bursts open.

'Come here, you little cunts,' a man's voice yells. 'We're coming to get you.'

Little children are dragged from their hiding places. Punched. Kicked. Lifted by arms, feet, hair, any body part the monsters can grab hold of. Some are small enough to carry. Others are dragged away by their hair. Then one comes for me. Looming large, with hatred in his eyes.

'Get here, you little bastard.'

I swing my blade as my heart bangs like a drum.

'Fuck off!' I scream, my fist clenched around the knife, stabbing the air between us. 'I'll stab you! Leave me alone!'

He moves closer until I can smell beer on his breath and my whole body trembles with terror. He reaches for me as I stab harder, daring him to touch me, and then his evil gaze turns to a boy quivering on the floor by my bed.

'Fuck off!' I scream once more as I watch him turn and suddenly grab the little boy, who's crying, eyes as wide as saucers. His piercing screams echo down the hallway as he's dragged away...

My eyes snap open and for a split second I don't know where I am. A familiar film of sweat is covering me. I put a hand on my chest to calm my breathing.

'It's okay, it's okay.'

My wife, Jo, is sitting up beside me. Her worried face is next to mine, her smooth palm on my forehead. Straight away I start to apologise, just like I've done a million times before, just like I will probably do again, but she shushes me and tells me it was just a dream. Just another broken night's sleep thanks to me and my past.

I put a hand on my chest where my physical scars still exist, reassuring myself I am back in my fifty-five-year-old man's body. I'm Paul Connolly again, a happily married father of two who needs to get up in a few hours for work as a personal trainer. I'm not the unwanted, unloved eight-year-old who existed in St Leonard's Children's Home in Hornchurch, Essex, living in fear for his life.

Rationally I know this was just a nightmare, but it feels so very real because well over forty years ago this did happen. We called these groups of men, who dragged us from our beds in the children's home to rape us, the Snatch Squads. And sometimes they still come for me in my sleep today.

Chapter 1: Into the Fire

When I was a two-week-old baby, my biological mother dumped me outside with the rubbish. Awful, right? But the truth is, by the time I learned of my sad beginnings, my self-esteem was so low, it didn't feel that bad. By then I'd already worked out what neglect was. The dark pain it causes, worse than any beatings. I'd lived through so much, meeting so many abusive adults along the way, that how my life began barely mattered.

Let me go back to what I do remember. After our next-door neighbours found me on top of bin bags, I was taken to St Vincent's Orphanage in Mill Hill, London. There, I spent the first four years of my life being looked after in a nursery by nuns. I have few memories, but those that I do have were okay. Happy even. One eighteen-year-old nursery nurse called Mary took a shine to me. She was a gentle, kind lady with a posh voice like the Queen's, who wore her hair up in a sixties-style do and looked a bit like Mary Quant.

'You're a special little boy, Paul,' she'd tell me. 'You're the seventh son of a seventh son, and that means you're lucky, you know.'

I didn't know what she was on about, but later I learned my dad was one of seven boys and I was the seventh boy too. In Irish folklore, and other cultures too, that means you're born lucky. Although for a long time, I felt anything but lucky.

'Mary, can you be my mum?' I used to ask her as soon as I was old enough to know what a 'mum' was.

'Paul, I would if I could,' she'd say. Later on, I learned she'd tried to adopt me, but my birth mother refused to sign the forms to allow this.

Mary filled in the gaps about my birth family. They were from Connemara, Ireland, originally; my mum was a midwife and my dad was a builder. They moved to London before I was born, and that's when things fell apart. I was the youngest of eight kids, and we were all put into care, apart from me. I got put out with the bin bags.

'But your dad was a good man,' Mary reassured me. 'He tried to keep your family together.'

Apparently, he even came to visit a couple of times too, although I only have vague memories of this. My siblings, from oldest to youngest, were Anne, Mick, Matty, Peter, Declan, Danny, John and then me. But, sent to different places, never to reunite, we were all so damaged that a normal sibling relationship became impossible. Mary would try to encourage me to see John, who was in the older boys' part of St Vincent's, from time to time, even though he never seemed to want to play with me. I met all my siblings later on, but we were strangers rather than brothers and sister.

At St Vincent's there were mean nuns who would give you a whack, but they were mainly kind to us. Every Christmas we got a present from the local factory; every Easter they brought a massive chocolate egg and a nun hit it with a mallet, and then they let us grab the sweets that fell to the floor. They organised football matches for us and they had allotments where they grew vegetables for home-cooked meals. Best of all, every summer Mary would whisk me away to her home on the south coast. Even after she left St Vincent's and got married to a man called Adrian, for one whole week a year she'd treat me like her own son, buying me clothes and feeding me up. I loved her more than anyone.

Aside from what Mary told me, the Connolly family remained a mystery. My only clue was the strange woman who would come to St Vincent's to visit once a year. I'd be taken to a room and she'd stick her head in briefly, say 'Hello' and then 'Goodbye' and leave.

'That was your mum,' a nun would say. But I didn't know the woman from Adam.

It turned out my birth mum had to visit at least once every twelve months specifically to stop me being adopted. This decision meant I would never find a loving family or have a real home. God knows why she decided to do this, as she wasn't interested in looking after me either.

*

Aged five, I had to say goodbye to the comfort of the nursery and Mary and move to the big boys' dormitory. There was a strict timetable now and the nuns were tougher. The beds were so high I could barely reach them and there was a huge shower block, no baths.

That first night I cried myself to sleep as I felt so alone. This was the first taste of a loneliness that was to colour everything. Around this time, my unsettling nightmares began. I can't tell you what happened. I'd not yet even met the real monsters, but as a tiny kid you can sense insecurity and unhappiness. The nuns did their best, but we were still small children and we needed real love.

Looking back, I can see we were crazy at times. One of my clearest memories is of jumping from one windowsill to another about three storeys high. One slip and we would have had it. I don't know if we didn't understand the dangers or didn't care. We'd been taught to fear God rather than the real world, perhaps.

Then, after two more summers passed, I was told it was time for me to leave St Vincent's for good.

'When you're eight you move to a new home,' a nun explained. 'A lovely place in the countryside called St Leonard's.'

And sure enough, a few weeks before my birthday, a man in a suit who reminded me of Sidney Poitier turned up to take me. I don't remember saying goodbye to Mary – maybe I've blanked it out – but she promised me we'd keep in touch. So I set off for the train station with all my worldly belongings, about three items of clothing, in a suitcase with this man, Mr Gardener.

'You're going to a new place where your brothers live, John, Declan and Danny,' he said. 'Won't that be nice?'

I nodded. I barely knew John, but perhaps Declan and Danny might like me? I'd heard Peter had once lived there too, another brother I'd never met.

We got a taxi from the train station and Mr Gardener held open the door at the end of what appeared to be a very long driveway. Small brick houses lined the drive at either side, and there were fields everywhere.

'Here we are, Paul,' he said. 'There are thirteen cottages where around thirty children sleep with a house parent. There's a theatre, a football pitch, playing fields, even an orchard.'

That sounded exciting. Maybe I was lucky after all? But as we wandered up the driveway I saw just how big the old buildings were, like somewhere I might get lost. Later I learned St Leonard's had been built in the Victorian times in what was green countryside near London. The idea was to give unwanted children a healthy life in beautiful greenery. Instead it turned out to be a place of hell, tucked safely away from Tower Hamlets Council who were supposed to be running the place and yet didn't appear to have a clue what was going on – or, worse, did know and turned a blind eye.

'Alright,' I replied, not knowing what to say. Any sense of excitement was being replaced by something else.

Fear.

I'd been taken away from everything I'd ever known. Already I wanted to go back.

*

We walked for what seemed like ages until we stopped at my cottage. 'It's called Forbes Cottage,' said Mr Gardener, letting go of my hand. Then a couple appeared at the door. The man looked huge – middle-aged, with a fat stomach and a stubbly black beard. He looked down at me.

'This is Bill Starling and this is Coral. You call your house parents "Uncle" and "Auntie" here,' Mr Gardner explained.

Auntie and Uncle? I'd never had an auntie or uncle before.

Auntie Coral was younger, a dark-haired woman wearing tight, blue jeans. They both stared down without smiling.

'Okay, come in,' she said eventually. Neither of them made me feel welcome.

I'm just another kid to them, I thought.

They led me upstairs to a long hallway where two dormitories ran off the sides, one for girls and one for boys, with the staff quarters in the middle.

'Dinner is at five,' said Auntie Coral. I looked at her face, hoping to spot some kindness. Already I missed Mary's smiling face.

That night I sat on a long bench with the other kids, who all clamoured for the food when it arrived. We were having beans and Spam fritters, and it was put on my plate quickly.

Slop. Slop.

There was only a small amount, so I ate it quickly, hoping for seconds like everyone else, but there were none. I looked down the long table at all the new thin, pale faces and wanted to cry. I knew nobody. Then someone pushed Declan in front me.

'Here's your brother,' someone said.

This boy stared at me. He didn't look like I'd imagined my brother to look. He had dark hair like mine, but that was it. He didn't smile or hug me, he just shrugged.

'I'll tell you who to look out for,' he said. 'Tell you who to worry about. Alan Prescott is the deputy head. He's a nasty vicious bastard, as is Bill Starling, so keep away from them, alright?'

I had no idea what a 'vicious bastard' was, but I was very soon to find out. Then Declan also told me about Peggy, nicknamed Wooden Tit for the prosthetic boob she had after suffering from cancer. He liked her. But, worse luck, she had left and there were no nice house parents left apparently. I watched Declan walk off after our quick chat, knowing there was little bond between us.

Later, I met Danny and John, my older brothers by six years and two years. They didn't make me feel any more welcome.

'Alright, Paul,' they both said.

They're my brothers, but I don't know them, I thought sadly.

Peter, another brother, was sixteen and had already left the home before I arrived. *Maybe*, I thought, *one day we'd all get to know each other*.

It didn't take long before I understood exactly what Declan meant. Alan Prescott was a short, stocky man with a hard stare from his piercing blue eyes. He was always touching the kids in ways that gave me the creeps, when he wasn't shouting at us. Starling was even worse. That afternoon I saw him give backhanders for the slightest thing. Aside from the odd smack from a nun, I'd never been hit before, so I wanted to avoid these two men as much as possible.

There were kids from everywhere here; big, menacing kids to small, frightened-looking ones. Other kids talked about rent boys too, not that I understood what they did, but they were in 'for their own protection'. There were lots of black and mixed-raced kids here, and Irish like me. Society was against all these groups in the 1970s, with landlords even being allowed to put signs in their windows saying 'No Blacks, No Irish, No Dogs'. And we were the unwanted kids of these much-hated groups of people, so ultimately we were the lowest of the low – and boy, were we made to feel this. The house parents always called us names I'd never heard before, like *cunt*, *scum*, *fucker*, *shit*, and other swearwords I'd never have dared use in front of the nuns. All our aunties and uncles seemed to hate the kids. I wondered why. Maybe the kids were naughtier here than at St Vincent's?

I quickly realised something else too. Vicious fights started at the slightest thing and the staff didn't tolerate anything. Any hint of trouble and staff came steaming in, walloping the kids really hard, slapping their faces, punching their noses and kicking even little legs. Especially Starling and Prescott. They couldn't seem to get enough of it.

That night I pulled on my scratchy new stripy pyjamas. My tummy hurt with hunger and I wanted to cry, but no tears came. I'd never felt so alone in the world, and deep down I knew very well there was absolutely nobody to save me.

*

The next thing I remember I woke, feeling damp. Just as I opened my eyes a woman's twisted, angry face was in mine.

'Get up, you little Irish cunt. You've pissed the bed, you revolting shit.'

That woman, Auntie Coral, roughly pulled me to my feet and half dragged me to the bathroom. I shivered as I pulled off my wet bottoms. She'd already run a bath and it stank of chemicals.

'Get in, you dirty Irish shit,' she said, pushing me and my soggy bed sheets into the bath.

The icy water took my breath away. 'But it's f-f-freezing,' I began to cry.

'This'll teach you,' she shrieked. She got out a scrubbing brush and, with force, made contact with my body. She seemed furious, a rage I'd never felt towards me before and my mind was racing.

'What have I done so wrong?'

'Why is someone who is supposed to care for me treating me like this?'

'Where is this anger from...?'

'I know who you are,' she snarled at me. 'You're another one of those Connolly boys. Irish lowlifes, the lot of you. I know your sort. Already I've had it with your brothers, Peter, John, Declan, and now you! Well, this will fucking teach you the first lesson. Don't wet the bed, you little cunt.'

'Ow, ow,' I gasped. She was scrubbing with such force, my skin began to tear. She only paused to pour more bleach in.

'Oi, shut your mouth. If you were normal, you would have a mum and dad who love you. But you're not normal and that's why nobody does! No point in crying like a baby.'

She lifted up my arms, scrubbing underneath, and then my neck, my back, my backside and my legs until I felt like my whole body was on fire. It seemed to go on forever. Only when my body was covered in red marks did she seem satisfied.

'Now. Get. Out!' she screamed.

She roughly dried me before flinging a white shirt and grey trousers at me. 'Get dressed in your school uniform. You're not to be late for the bus.'

I slowly pulled on my clothes, wincing with every move. I did up the buttons and spotted red flecks of blood soaking through. *Would I be in trouble for this too?*

Afterwards, I stuffed down some stale toast before running outside for the bus to take me for my first day at my new school, St Mary's Catholic Junior School. I climbed aboard and sat in the empty seat next to an older boy. He raised an eyebrow at me. For a split second his eyes flickered to the blood on my shirt, but he did not mention it.

'Alright? I'm Liam,' he said, winking. 'Don't fucking worry about this starting school shit. Anyone fucks with you; you're with me, okay? They try and fuck with all us lot from the home all the fucking time there, but I won't fucking have it. Okay?'

Cor, I thought. *This blond kid swears a lot.*

But I was grateful for Liam. This tough kid was offering to be my minder, the first kind thing anyone had done for me since I'd arrived. I managed to smile and he smiled back. He looked much older than me and I liked his cockiness.

'Hiya, Liam,' I said. 'I'm Paul.'

We chatted all the way there. Never about our pasts – nobody spoke about that – just about schools and what subjects we hated. Neither of us could read, and Liam said all the teachers were wankers.

'But sit next to me and I'll show you what's what,' he grinned.

I hadn't been to school much – we barely went to any classes at St Vincent's – but I was old enough to understand that kids from care homes weren't liked by normal kids from normal families. We wore cheap uniforms, had bad haircuts, got free school meals and had no mum or dad. We might as well have gone to school with a big target sign on our heads.

By the end of that first day, me and my mate were inseparable. I had no idea what Liam saw in me. He had his own posse who didn't take shit from anybody. But he got me straight off and we made each other laugh. I didn't get this at the time, but Liam taught me that nature wins over nurture. He'd received very little love in his life but he had a big heart.

Looking back, I guess Liam recognised me as an abused kid straight away. Also, later on I realised there was a reason he had a seat to himself on that bus. Most kids were intimidated by him, so they left him alone.

Chapter 2: True Horror

Within days of arriving at St Leonard's, I'd seen more violence than I'd seen in my entire life. Never knowing when the next punch or kick would happen, I walked on eggshells, avoiding staff and staying close to Liam when I could. Anything could be used as a weapon too. Kids walked around with penknives, stones and clenched fists, while staff who smoked often used their burning fag-ends on bare legs to shut kids up.

That first Saturday, I was in the day room when a kid called Steve complained about someone changing the channel on the black-and-white TV. Within seconds of the row, a staff member called Colin charged in like a raging bull and, without even listening to anyone, started punching the boy with all his strength. After Steve fell to the floor, Colin picked up the TV and threw it on top of him. Then he left Steve crying.

I had never met so many grownups who were so angry all of the time. By the end of the weekend, I'd seen Uncle Bill punish kids by punching them up the stairs, step by step, and then kicking them down again, and I also saw several little boys get thrown against walls with full force. I had never seen a grown man use his full physical strength against a small child before. It was terrifying.

A week or so later, Auntie Coral and Uncle Bill told us we were being moved to a new cottage called Wallis.

'You lot are all coming with us,' Bill grinned.

The way he said it made me shiver.

My instincts proved to be right, as the violence got worse now that Auntie Coral and Uncle Bill were on their own with thirty kids. Auntie Coral never missed a chance to shout at me. Every morning when I woke up she'd begin.

'You're just a cunt, Paul Connolly. Connolly the Cunt. Do you know why you're here? It's because nobody loves you. You don't have a proper family, you just have us. Now get out of bed and get dressed, and do as I say,' she'd say.

Sometimes she went further and made it even more personal. 'You just got thrown out in the rubbish because that's what you are,' could be the first words I heard in the morning.

I didn't cry or tell her to stop, I just listened. My brain absorbed her words like a sponge, as that's what happens when you're a kid. You believe whatever it is you're told, and now on a daily basis I was told this: You're unwanted and unloved and worth nothing.

The only good thing was that my new cottage was opposite Myrtle Cottage where Liam lived, so we could wave to each other before lights out. It was very comforting, seeing him last thing every night, his face pressed against the frosted, old glass window, smiling at me. I can still see him waving to me now.

'Night, Paul,' I imagined him saying.

'Night, Liam,' I would say aloud as I lingered over seeing his friendly face before lights out.

After the first few weeks of school, me and Liam were good mates and I was a fast learner of my new vocabulary. Nobody stopped me swearing anymore. I loved hanging out with my new friend, cussing and laughing at people before they had a chance to laugh at us – the boys from St Leonard's. Neither of us could read, so we were just a pair of little fuckers to the teachers. But we were in this together, me and Liam against the world. Turned out we were both born in August, me on the second and him on the twenty-first, and we were both Irish Catholics. Liam had lived at St Leonard's from the age of three and had four brothers. He never told me why he was in care, like I never told him, as there was no point. This was our life and we had to deal with it. I was just grateful that now I had someone like him to do it with together.

*

Bill didn't just use his fists; he also made us feel bad by eating food in front of us while we starved. He'd sit with a big plate of Edam cheese slices and fat chip-shop chips, stuff we never got to touch, and slowly eat it in front of us as we got ready for bed.

'Hmm, this is tasty,' he'd grin. 'Shame none of you little bastards can have any, isn't it?'

Having to watch him savour food was torture. I realised something else too. Here was a grownup who took pleasure in our torment.

You're a total bastard, I thought. I had never hated an adult as much as I hated him.

That summertime, we were put to bed at seven p.m. despite it being light outside still, so kids often mucked about at bedtime. But now that Uncle Bill and Auntie Coral had a cottage to themselves, the punishments became more frightening. Then one evening, soon after we moved, they returned with friends, all drunk and shouting at us to get into the hallway. We all got out of bed and I saw kids running down the hallway, looking panicked, all of them taking off their tops and pyjama bottoms on the stairs, almost tripping over one another. I stared in confusion as I saw all their private parts.

Why are the kids undressing in such a hurry? I thought. *Why are the adults making them?*

As the kids all stood to attention next to the wall, I joined them and slowly started taking my top off. I was embarrassed. I didn't like this. Then Uncle Bill started to tell us what to do.

'Stand on one leg,' he barked.

We all did as he said and I realised something. This had happened before to these kids. The strangers laughed at us, shoving a few kids so they lost their balance.

'Look at you, all your pathetic little dicks on show,' Uncle Bill yelled.

He kicked one boy, aged about ten, in the nuts and the boy doubled over, crying.

Seconds turned into minutes and some kids' legs wobbled, but if they tried to put a foot down Uncle Bill screamed at them. Then he shouted at one little boy to lift his leg higher. As he did so, Uncle Bill kicked the other leg from beneath him and he collapsed onto the floor.

'Get up, you little shit,' he yelled, dragging him up by his hair.

The little boy started crying, but the strangers were laughing. Then Bill punched the boy in the face so he fell backwards and huddled into a ball on the floor. The strangers all jeered, encouraging Uncle Bill, who then kicked the kid to the ground as he started to get up. Then, to my horror, he unzipped his trousers.

'I need a piss,' he laughed as he pulled out his maggot-like penis and he began to pee on the boy's head.

We all watched in silence. The smell of Uncle Bill's piss made me feel sick. The little boy sobbed as he was left lying, soaked and naked. *Humiliated.*

Back then I didn't know what the word 'humiliation' meant, but that night I learned it.

'Right, you little cunts. GET TO BED!' Uncle Bill screamed.

And we all ran back to our beds, scooping up our pyjamas on the way. But sleeping was impossible. I tossed and turned, unable to relax. After all, I never knew what was going to happen next and I was already dreading waking up.

*

When I first arrived, the home was run by a guy called Datner who was a former RAF fighter pilot. With his military connections, every year he put up a group of kids for an international one-hundred-mile march in Holland, called the Nijmegen March. This was a four-day event involving armies and representatives from all around the world, including kids from homes. If you were chosen, you had to train every weekend and be part of a group to go abroad. Liam and I really wanted to go, and I vowed one day I would. Unlike our house parents, Datner seemed like an okay guy. I never saw him being abusive to kids, but then again I wonder now what he saw while he was there. He told us kids he never slept for more than fifteen minutes at night-time, something the boys would try to catch him out with, but they never did.

There were so many staff who worked at St Leonard's; aside from the house parents, there were shift workers and cleaners and cooks – so many adults coming and going all the time. But I soon realised something else was going on too. The kids who had parents who came to visit, or anyone else from the outside interested in their welfare, got treated differently to boys like me and Liam, who had nobody to visit or care for them.

For example, the Morris twins, Lenny and Tony, whose parents came and sat in the kitchen to chat to them every week or so, were given fish fingers and mash for dinner. They were also allowed more sweets and were not hit as much. But then there were these twin girls, Susie and Sonia, aged about ten, who were allowed into Uncle Bill and Auntie Coral's room to watch the colour TV and given crisps, even though they didn't have parents. I couldn't understand why. It seemed so unfair. I thought it might be because they were pretty. Only later did I understand the price they paid for those treats.

A few of the boys in my dorm were always being pulled in and out of the room by staff too. Leeroy was a mixed-race kid who had suffered from polio and limped everywhere. He was very quiet; he reminded me of a ghost at times. Then there was Mark Byrnes, a ginger kid who I didn't think was too bright. Neither of them had parents who visited and they'd often disappear into staff quarters.

Then one day Leeroy and Mark returned to bed, their pyjama bottoms off and blood dripping onto the floor. I felt sorry for them but didn't know what had happened. Then someone told me Auntie Coral fucked my brother, Peter, who was sixteen. Then someone said house parents liked to fuck the kids. I didn't even know what 'fucking' was. All I knew was I didn't want to go to bed crying and bleeding like Leeroy and Mark.

With all this upset around me I was desperate for any distraction, and thankfully Liam was keen to have me in his world outside St Leonard's. My friend was so smart, hard and fearless. He didn't take any shit from anyone, and it meant people left him alone. I began to look up to Liam like I'd never done with anyone else before. He was always coming up with ideas for how to fill our hungry bellies too.

One Saturday afternoon he suggested we went and got some fish and chips.

'But I don't have any money, Liam,' I said.

He just laughed at me. 'Don't you fucking worry about that,' he said.

There were always games of poker going on in the home, usually with the older kids, so I wondered if Liam had won on there. I didn't dare ask him. We wandered down to the chip shop, where the shopkeeper recognised Liam.

'Hello, boys. What can I get you today?' he asked.

'Chips, mate,' said Liam.

'Salt? Vinegar?'

'Both,' Liam replied.

'What's the word for that?' said the shopkeeper, looking at us suspiciously.

Liam wrinkled his nose and rolled his eyes. He was always like this around adults; he had no respect for them. The chippie geezer bunged a load of fish batter set for the bin into our wrap anyway. He must have felt sorry for us, a rare thing, as usually to the outside world we were just poor kids from the home.

'Thanks,' I said to him as we left for the fields.

On the way, Liam popped into a bakery and swiped a loaf of bread when nobody was looking. We sat on a tree stump, scooped out the inside of the bread and filled it with chips. We tore into our food so fast it gave us indigestion. Satisfied to have a full stomach for once, we lay back in the grass.

'One day I'll fucking kill that cunt Uncle Bill,' said Liam suddenly. 'Fucking strangle him or something.'

I loved that idea.

'I'll help you,' I said. 'You do Bill. I'll do Coral.' We both laughed, lost in our fantasy about what we'd do to all the bastards.

After that, we often disappeared in the evenings and at weekends to find something extra. We nicked milk off people's doorsteps, apples from trees or sweets from the newsagents. Anything to stop the gnawing hunger.

Because we were two of the few Catholics from the home, we also had to go to confession together. Even as a little boy, the religion meant nothing to me. We were told to confess our sins and do all that Hail Mary stuff, but then we'd go back to our school with mean teachers and our home with horrible carers. The Church didn't give a stuff about us; that was all we learned about that damn religion. Years later, when I learned how against birth control the Catholics are too, my anger grew. They didn't stop babies being born, but then they refused to help look after them or stop them from being abused. What a bunch of fucking hypocritical scum! But anyway, we were expected to go and confess our sins every week without fail, like good little Catholics.

One morning the following spring, we were on our way there, wondering what to confess.

'What you gonna say?' Liam asked.

'Dunno. We've not done much,' I began. 'Only played Knock-up Ginger and stolen a couple of things from the newsagents.'

'Maybe we should do something worse then? C'mon, I fancy a lemonade,' Liam said. I didn't know what he was on about, but then he nodded towards the Corona factory nearby.

'Genius,' I laughed.

We were always craving sugar as we were so hungry all the time, so of course we fancied a few bottles of fizz. We climbed over the wall, dropped down the other side and found crates of glass bottles. Carrying a crate back over the wall between us, we thought we'd made it. Then we heard a man shout.

'Oi, you two. What the fuck's going on?'

I was about to drop the crate but Liam winked at me. 'Let's take it with us,' he said.

Between us we carried the crate, half jogging away. It was ridiculous, but I loved how Liam refused to drop it and give up.

'We're faster than them cunts anyway,' Liam grinned. But as I looked over my shoulder, I saw not one but about ten men.

'Er, Liam,' I began.

He swung around.

'Oh, shit!' he yelled.

I began to let go of my side of the crate, but Liam held on to his.

'I ain't running,' he grinned at me.

'Then I ain't running either, Liam.'

Instead he picked up a bottle of the pop and lobbed it in the direction of the workers. One ducked and it smashed on the ground, fizzing into the concrete. I laughed and threw another one. Soon bottle after bottle sailed through the air at the grownups, who were cussing and diving to avoid them.

'I ain't running, Paul,' repeated Liam, still giggling.

'Then I ain't fucking running either then,' I yelled over the noise of the glass.

The men, angrier than ever, were getting closer and closer, but with Liam by my side I began to feel less scared. I just had to pretend to be as fearless as my friend. Then I lobbed one last bottle, before losing my own bottle, and I turned to leg it.

'C'mon, Liam, they'll kill us! We gotta go!'

I started running for my life, the men only metres away.

'Hahahaha!' Liam yelled at my back. 'Told ya you'd run before me.'

Then he spun around and joined me, soon overtaking because he was so much faster. We collapsed in nearby woodland, having lost the puffing and panting men after a few minutes, and we couldn't stop laughing.

'Got loads to confess about to our Mother Mary now,' Liam laughed.

From then on we were a team; Liam always taking the lead, with me close behind like his shadow. We sneaked off as often as possible, away from the misery of the home to nearby fields. One of our favourite places to go was The Chase, a piece of wasteland near a factory. In this field we found horses grazing peacefully and we felt drawn to them.

As we approached them I saw a change in Liam. He stopped swearing and used a softer voice. One was a big brown-and-white Shire horse, a massive thing.

''Ere, boy, I won't hurt ya,' Liam soothed.

The horse moved towards us, nuzzling its velvety nose into our faces as we laughed.

'He knows we won't hurt him,' I said.

We stood and stroked the horses for ages.

'Wonder who owns them?' Liam said.

'Maybe they don't belong to anyone,' I suggested. 'Just like us.'

We left them that day vowing to come back soon.

Returning to St Leonard's always made us feel shit. There was always a row going on, or one of the bigger kids making the little ones cry or fighting them. But nothing prepared me for what was to happen this particular Saturday night. This was the beginning of a nightmare that was to haunt me for years to come. All the staff went off to The Harrow, a pub opposite, and at first I thought this was great. It meant we had some peace and quiet from the staff and could do what we liked for a change. But some kids began to fret and pace the room. Others just huddled in their beds, shaking. One or two started to stare out of the window, looking jumpy.

'What's going on?' I asked.

'Snatch Squad,' said someone quietly.

I began to feel really uneasy. I didn't ask what he meant. I didn't want to know.

By eleven p.m., some kids had started to cry, while others had begun to crawl under their beds. Two younger boys who had been on the lookout at the window since about ten p.m. ran off to hide too.

'They're coming!'

'Shit!'

All of a sudden kids started clamouring to get away, hiding anywhere they could, which was basically just under the beds or in wardrobes. At first I sat on my bed scared stiff. Then I pulled my thin blanket over me, pretending I didn't exist.

Something awful was about to happen, but I didn't know what.

I saw their shadows at the window first of all. They reminded me of the masked IRA men I'd seen on the news, as they ran one by one, like soldiers, up the fire escape, right where my bed was. Then the door burst open and terrified screams rose into the air.

'Come here, you little cunts!' cried a voice sounding like Uncle Bill's from behind the mask.

He was followed by a group of strangers, all in balaclavas, who started chasing kids around the room. Some ran like hell to the corners of the room, while others were dragged from their hiding places. Some kids kicked as they were carried away, others went limp and sobbed. I jumped onto my mattress as a man in a mask ran towards me. I turned to move but he lifted me by the waist.

'Get here, you little shit,' he yelled.

I started to kick and twist my body, wriggling like mad. I didn't know what he wanted, but this obviously wasn't some kind of game. Every kid around me seemed petrified.

He held me with one arm as he tried to scoop up another boy, so I twisted my torso and kicked hard until he had to let go. Then I leapt back onto my bed, my back against the wall, trembling.

My resistance appeared to put him off because he started to pick up a kid who was shaking with fear on the floor.

Then I heard one of the staff yell at another one. 'Not him. Drop him, take another one instead!' This made me realise some kids were safe. It seemed to be the kids who had parents that came to visit them who were safe from being grabbed.

I felt sick to my stomach. By now all the men had one or two kids in their arms, dragging them off to the staff quarters. Then the door slammed and the blood-curdling screaming continued behind it. I lay on the bed, pillow over my head, unable to bear it. Sounds of men yelling, kids being thumped and then more screaming. Some of the screams became more muffled, while other screams pierced the walls and seemed to go on forever.

After half an hour, kids returned in dribs and drabs. Some were silent, others cried, others just looked dazed, and all of them were bleeding from their bottoms and in pain. It was about an hour before they were all back in bed. All of us cried ourselves to sleep and nobody comforted anyone. We were all too lost in our own worlds of pain.

That night, as I cried myself to sleep silently, I felt so alone it physically hurt. I couldn't understand what kind of place this was, but if I'd understood what it meant, I'd have said it was hell on earth and there was nobody in the world to save me.

Chapter 3: Survival

That next night I waited until everyone was asleep before sneaking into the kitchen. I knew I had to find a weapon to protect myself. According to the kids in my dormitory, the Snatch Squads were a regular thing and the last thing I wanted was for the men to pick on me. As scared as I was, I slipped out of our dorm and tiptoed past the staff quarters door, being careful not to wake Uncle Bill or Auntie Coral. Then I slid outside, across the courtyard to the kitchen quarters, where I opened the door and ran inside. I crawled on my belly across the linoleum floor and quickly opened a few kitchen drawers. It didn't take long to find what I was looking for. I tucked a small kitchen knife up my sleeve and slipped back to the dormitory, where I quickly hid it underneath the floorboards. Just knowing it was there made me feel safer.

It didn't take long before I needed my new friend; my knife. Just two weeks later, the Snatch Squad burst in just like they had before, but this time I had something to protect me. I wasn't quite ready when they arrived, so I found myself scrabbling under the bed like my life depended on it as a masked man tried to grab me.

I thought my heart might burst from my ribcage as I tore at the floorboards in panic.

'C'mon here,' the man yelled, his mouth full of spittle. 'Do as you're told!'

'Fuck off! Fuck off!' I screamed, clawing at the wood. Finally it came away in my hand and I was able to grab the knife with the other one just as he reached my bed.

My whole body trembled as I circled the knife in front of me, daring him to come closer, but he didn't. He turned and reached for one of the kids, who was frozen to the spot with fear. He picked him up and carried him off under his arm like a prize animal. I carried on waving my knife in the air until all the men disappeared and the screaming started next door.

Then I lay back down, breathing as if I'd run a marathon, sweat running down my back.

You have to fight them off, I thought. *You have to use your knife all the time now. It's the only way they'll leave you alone.*

Just like last time, all the kids returned sobbing or white as ghosts, bleeding and dazed. That night I slept clutching the knife under my pillow.

*

By now I had met most of the boys who became my friends for the next ten years of my life. Michael, Mark Byrnes, Frank Carr, Leeroy, George, Danny and Lawrence.

Michael was a confident black kid who made everyone laugh. As the joker of the pack, he loved to wind people up just for the heck of it. Lawrence was a smoothie for such a young boy. He liked to dress as well as he could and was crazy about girls from a very young age. Frank was a strange kid. He was very effeminate and over all the years we were in the home he was teased relentlessly for being a girl. George and Mark were the ones who later on, as teens, became addicted to glue-sniffing. Whereas Leeroy, a skinny mixed-race disabled kid, was hard to get to know. He often limped around like a husk of a person. That's what seemed to happen if you were one of the staff's favourites. Danny was a nice black kid too, with a big afro and a wide smile. We didn't chat much and he was pretty shy, but everyone liked him.

For the first few months, I was learning fast how to survive each day as it came. My knife became my protector and Liam became a guru to me. His anger went from zero to one-hundred within milliseconds if anyone gave him any grief, so I copied him. I wanted people to fear me like they did him; to be known as the kid no one dared to mess with, even if it didn't feel natural at first and even if I was a small, skinny boy compared to Liam. Truth was, I didn't know what I was doing or who I was, just that I didn't want to be dragged from my bed and returned with a bleeding bum.

But with my newfound bravado it wasn't long before my first run-in with Uncle Bill.

It was another long evening after being sent to bed in the daylight. In they came, Uncle Bill and some boozed-up friends. Thankfully none of them were wearing balaclavas, so we knew it wasn't a Snatch Squad, but they lined us up in the hallway again – naked. I hated the way they spoke to us all, like we were pieces of shit. But I especially hated the stupid games they played with us. Getting us to stand on one leg like flamingos or to jump up and down. So when Uncle Bill asked us to do the flamingo, barking like a sergeant major, I just picked up my leg for a second before putting it back down.

'Oi, Connolly, fucking lift it back up again,' he yelled. I lifted it again and put it down a second later. He noticed.

'Up, I said!' he snarled into my face.

I lifted it up, but as soon as he walked off again, I put it down. He turned and noticed.

'Oh, right, I see, Paul. You're going to be a clever little cunt, are you?' he said, lighting a fag. 'Right, come here.'

I hated standing naked in front of everyone, all of them staring at me, but something inside of me felt I had to do this. I wasn't going to just accept whatever he told us anymore. It wasn't right.

He sucked in on his cigarette, making the end glow, and then exhaled an acrid puff of smoke.

'Put your foot down,' he snapped. But I shook my head.

Then, without warning, he bent down and pushed his fag butt deep into my chest. The pain made me gasp and I fell backwards into the wall, but he kept pressing it. My small pigeon chest was being used as a human ashtray. I shrieked out as the cigarette seared into me. The smell of my burning flesh and his stale tobacco reached my nose.

'Still want to be a clever little cunt, do you?' he snapped as I fell to the floor. 'DO YOU?'

I clutched my chest, unable to stop the tears streaming down my face.

'Get up, Paul Connolly, and do as I say. I said: GET UP!'

I scrabbled to my feet, aware of everyone's eyes on me. Some kids were crying but most were silent.

'Now stand on one leg,' he grinned.

I did this, sobbing my eyes out and clutching my chest, which burned like hell. Then, laughing his head off, he kicked my other leg from under me and I fell to the floor again. Crying, I covered my face, feeling so alone as I heard the sound of a trouser zipper going down. Then I felt piss being sprayed all over me, my head, my hair, my back and my chest. The pain was unbearable.

'Now get the fuck to bed,' he ordered, and laughed as all the kids ran off.

I managed to get to my feet, pushing wet hair from my face. I huddled in bed, still holding my chest, the overpowering stench of Uncle Bill's piss making me want to be sick. All I could do was hold the handle of my knife under the pillow. Just knowing it was there gave me more comfort than any cuddly toy ever could.

The next morning, Auntie Coral shoved me in the direction of the sick bay. 'That needs stitches,' she said, eyeing my chest. St Leonard's had its own mini hospital on-site and the nurses did a quick job of stitching it up.

'Ooh, the burn has gone right down to the bone,' one observed. But nobody asked how it happened. Or who did it. Nobody was interested. I still have that burn scar on my chest, forty-eight years later, but of course it's not just the physical scars from St Leonard's I still carry.

As always, Liam cheered me up. I never told him what happened exactly, as I didn't want him to think I couldn't take care of myself. Instead, we just escaped it all and went to see our horses, nicking a bottle of full-fat milk on the way. Feeling that creamy liquid slip down our throats was amazing for both of us. We were so hungry all the time, we were obsessed with food, and to feel temporarily full was the biggest treat. As we approached the brown-and-white horse, he came over.

'Think he knows who we are, don't you, boy?' Liam said.

I stroked the horse's mane, feeling like he understood us too.

'Come on, let's go for a ride,' Liam said.

'You what? Don't be crazy,' I began, knowing full well saying this would only egg Liam on. He was already pulling the horse to a tree so he could climb up it. It took a few goes but then he was on, high up, riding this horse bareback. Not to be outdone, I coaxed another friendly-looking horse over to a fence and climbed on. Both horses stood still as if waiting for what we wanted to do next. I patted my horse's mane, then gently kicked his side.

'Come on, boy,' I said.

We started trotting off side by side, laughing our heads off.

'You're the Indian, I'm the cowboy,' Liam yelled, kicking the horse so he sped up. I was scared we'd get thrown off, but both of our animals took it easy, as if they knew we were only little kids and needed to be protected.

After an hour or so, we stopped and jumped off. Then we spotted one of the workers from the factory who was wandering back from a shift.

''Ere, Mister. Do you know who these horses belong to?' asked Liam.

The worker shrugged. 'Nobody. They're all going off to be slaughtered for dog food,' he said before going on his way.

We stared at each other. I swear I saw Liam's eyes start to fill up. He sniffed loudly before giving his horse one last stroke.

'You're like us, ain't ya,' he whispered. 'You don't deserve none of this.'

*

Six months after I arrived, my social worker, called Celia Stock, turned up. She'd been my case worker since I was born, and now and then she'd drop in to ask how everything was going. If I'd been honest, I'd have told her it was a living hell and that Uncle Bill and his cronies were beating and raping kids as if that were normal. But of course I wasn't allowed to see her alone. Uncle Bill sat in the room next to me as she walked in. She sat down, ran her finger down the file and asked how I was.

'Fine,' I said, feeling Bill eyeballing me.

'You settled in okay?' she asked, not looking up.

'Yes, fine.'

'Made friends?'

'Yes,' I said, thinking of Liam and the others. This was the only honest answer I could give her.

'Oh, good,' she said, snapping her file shut. 'Thanks, Mr Starling, and I'll see you again in another six months' time.'

Bill followed her out, chatting in a pleasant-sounding voice, laughing and joking with her. It was a tone of voice he never used around us kids.

The only person I could consider telling what was happening was Mary. But I never did, and some people have questioned why. Well, let me explain. We kids were conditioned from a very young age never to tell and not to trust other adults. We were told they were all-powerful and we were lowlife cunts. Day in, day out. The result of this was the feeling it was pointless. If I did tell Mary, she might not believe me. And even if she *had* done, what would have happened? I saw social workers being fobbed off, and even other parents who very occasionally asked the question: *'Why has that child got so many bruises?'* And they got the same reply: *'Paul Connolly is a very violent little boy who is always in fights.'*

I still saw Mary very occasionally, and she was as kind and caring as ever. My time with Mary meant a longed-for break. I could finally relax at her place in the New Forest for the first time all year long. The last thing I wanted to do was speak about what was happening; I just lived in the moment, like most kids do.

This was against the background of the 1970s, when there was no such thing as whistle blowers. I don't believe all the staff were abusive, but even if they saw or suspected what went on behind closed doors, they couldn't tell as they'd lose their jobs. There were no tribunals back in those days. To be fair, I don't think the domestic staff were in on what was going on, as the abuse tended to be well hidden or stop when they were around. Often Auntie Coral or Uncle Bill would lower their voices or not give you a wallop when cleaners were on shift.

We kids knew the best time to use the bathroom was when it was cleaning time. The Mrs Mops who came to clean the toilets might have just been little old ladies in some cases, but being around them was the only form of protection we had. I believe the lower down the pecking order staff were in that home, the less likely they were to be involved with the abuse.

Not having anyone close to us meant that we kids were actually very immature and unable to cope with the world outside. Little things, like being taught to cross the road, passed us by, as nobody showed us how to do them. A few months after arriving, I was run over by a Vauxhall Chevette as I ran across the road to a sweet

shop to meet Liam. I just didn't see it coming and didn't think. The driver jumped out and shouted at me, before realising I could stand up, and then he drove off at speed. To him I was probably just another kid from the care home, damaged and unloved, so why should he care either? I quickly learned that was the usual reaction from the outside world. Lowlife Irish cunts, as Auntie Coral called us. After Liam helped pick me up, I limped back to my dormitory in tears, holding my arm as it hurt. Auntie Coral was already there and she eyed me suspiciously.

'What you done now?' she snapped.

'Just got run over,' I said. 'It really hurts.'

'You're so stupid, Connolly. Typical Irish, can't even learn how to cross the fucking road like a normal person.'

And that was all the sympathy I was getting.

School wasn't a place of care or safety either. In fact, all the teachers appeared to hate us. Looking back, I see we were little gits, always messing around and playing up. But Liam and I were both illiterate and the teachers didn't seem to acknowledge how behind we were or worry about our education. We'd always arrive at school starving hungry too and unable to concentrate. Often I'd have crippling headaches and my eyes would struggle to focus due to an empty belly. Only once did a teacher, called Mr Molloy, spot how badly bruised I was.

'Paul Connolly, will you look at you, you skinny little thing with all those bruises?' he said in his strong Northern Irish accent, 'What's been going on with you then?'

He turned up at the home the next day to speak to Uncle Bill. I was in the room as Uncle Bill eyeballed me, daring me to say a word.

'I wanted to ask about Paul Connolly and all the bruises he's showing up with,' Mr Molloy began. But Uncle Bill waved him away, pulling out my file. He thumbed through it and turned to the page on behaviour to show Molloy.

'Just take a look at one of Paul's reports. He's a very disturbed, violent little boy. He will even throw himself at the wall in a bid to get attention.'

Molloy began straining to read the words before Bill snapped the file shut abruptly.

'Sadly Connolly beats himself up,' he sighed, refusing to look at me. 'A very troubled individual he is. I fear for his future. You can tell he'll be going nowhere in life, but what can you do? We try our best, as I am sure you do.'

Molloy didn't seem to know how to respond to that. So that was that. He apologised for troubling Bill Starling, shook hands with him and never asked me about my bruises again.

Chapter 4: Revelations

Living in constant fear changes your body. When you can't ever relax, even at night-time, your body is flooded with adrenalin all the time. That's not normal and it's exhausting. Add constantly being hungry and quickly you feel pretty anxious and unwell. Although I was frightened, at the same time I couldn't ever show my fear. I had to force myself to pretend, as looking scared made you vulnerable.

After narrowly escaping the Snatch Squad, I'd realised that if I allowed myself to freeze in situations, I would get raped and hurt. But if I was very violent and fought back then the abusers left me alone. So I started carrying around my knife at all times. If a kid came too close, I would threaten them too. To prove how hard I was, I picked fights with older kids. Sometimes this backfired and I ended up hurt, but I became so used to bruises and punches, I began not to feel pain like I used to.

Now I understood my best friend, Liam, even more. He was an angry little boy and was respected for it, so that's what I longed for too. Slowly, without realising it, I started to copy him and develop my own persona: Paul Connolly, the little shit nobody messed with. I frowned like Liam, gritted my teeth like him and started to swear like a trooper too. It felt good, better than being a weak little boy scared of his own shadow anyway.

Looking back, I realise being violent was what saved me. There is something about the horror of sexual abuse I believe kids don't ever recover from. All neglect is terrible but being buggered or raped as a child seems impossible to overcome for many people. Although attempts were made to rape me, it never actually happened. I don't think I'd be here to tell the story if it had been done. Being able to anticipate violence wasn't always possible though, and my biggest fear was being surprised by it. This often happened when Uncle Bill set the big kids onto the little ones as a means to control them, and I hated this.

One evening I dashed into the bathroom to wash quickly. I had learned to go in there only when domestic staff were around, and thankfully I could see they were mopping the floors outside. Often staff took the little kids in there, pretending to wash them while they abused them. Someone told me Auntie Coral liked to fiddle with the little ones' private parts when they were put on the potty. Worse still, some of the kids liked having their bits touched, simply because they craved attention that much. Hard to understand if you've never encountered such neglect before, but when you never get any attention whatsoever as a child, any feels better than none. Thanks to the twisted adults we relied on, this was the twisted way poor kids were forced to think.

Anyway, on this particular evening I was leaning over a sink, washing my face, when Tommy Maloney, one of the big kids, came barging in. He thumped the back of my neck so hard I smashed my nose into the basin.

'That's from Uncle Bill,' he laughed.

'Fuck you!' I screamed at him, holding my bleeding nose.

'He says you've been a little cunt today,' Tommy shouted, before legging it to get fags off Uncle Bill.

Then and there I vowed never to do the staff's dirty work. Watching big kids bully little ones was horrible, and it was horrible to experience.

After a year at St Leonard's I was unrecognisable from the quiet boy who'd arrived. I carried a knife around with me at all times, I swore constantly and I was always on edge, always ready for trouble. Months merged into another year, and the monotony of life was only briefly broken up by Christmases. Some of the kids would go home, but us 'lifers' stayed. We were allowed to watch the Christmas films, and we actually got a Christmas dinner that for the first time all year left us feeling full up. Nobody ever marked anyone's birthdays. It was yet another sign that our existence in this world wasn't anything to celebrate.

*

By the age of ten, Liam and I had to be confirmed into the Catholic church. This was part of the rite of passage for Catholic kids – First Holy Communion, Holy Communion and then being confirmed. None of it meant anything to us, as the priest was just as disinterested in us as everyone else was. But we had to do it as we had 'Catholic' written in our social worker files and it was another box to be ticked. So we went through the charade and repeated the verses after the priest, not understanding what they meant in the slightest. Afterwards, to our surprise, we were picked as altar boys.

'Why did they do that?' laughed Liam as we walked back from church.

'I ain't got no idea,' I said. 'I guess they couldn't find any other mugs to do it.'

Anyway, a week later we were asked to go along to the priest's quarters to dress up and practise our new, meaningless role. Once inside, the priest left us to get dressed in our white altar-boy robes. We laughed our heads off as we pulled on the thick, long gowns, pretending to be ghosts as we did it. After we were dressed, we looked around the room, itching for mischief.

'Hey, wanna try the wine?' said Liam, spotting a glass bottle. I grabbed it from him and took a swig.

'Fucking hell, it tastes like shit,' I said as it burned my throat.

'Paul, shhhh, he'll wash your mouth out,' laughed Liam.

Like always, we had empty stomachs, so within seconds the wine went to our heads. Feeling giggly, we started lighting candles.

'I'll say a prayer for your bad soul, dear Paul,' Liam said, doing a perfect Irish accent like the priest.

'Jesus Christ, I thank you,' I joked back.

But instead of putting the candle in the holder, Liam lobbed it at me. Then he lit two, three more, so I went to light one myself.

'Let me do one,' I said, but he shoved me.

'Fuck off,' he laughed. Liam always liked to take control and I liked to let him too.

But this time we struggled, and we didn't notice a candle was knocked over.

Then Liam cried out, 'Oi, we've set the fucking church on fire!'

Between us, the tablecloth had gone up in flames. We just looked at each other and laughed. It was hysterical, the idea of burning a church down. Just then the priest rushed in. He looked horrified.

'Dear God, what's been going on in here?' he yelled. He ran to get water, shooing us away like flies.

'Let's get outta here,' cried Liam, so we bolted to the door and, laughing our heads off, ran back to the home.

We only grew quieter when we approached St Leonard's. As we arrived, Haydn was waiting for us.

'Connolly! Caroll! You're coming with me.'

He frogmarched us across the courtyard before stopping and pushing me towards the main building.

'Starling is waiting for you in the kitchen,' he smirked, before taking Liam off to Myrtle. Liam tried to swing his head around to catch my eye but got a clout around the ear.

I knew what was coming, so I didn't rush to find it. I hung around for a few moments before knocking on the kitchen door.

'Who is it?' Bill barked.

'Paul Connolly.'

The door was flung open and he shoved me to the ground. Then he took a fistful of hair and dragged me across the gravel. I felt other kids watching from the windows as he started to punch me with his full force, before throwing me at the wall. I landed in a heap, my head spinning as blows and kicks came from everywhere. It was all happening so fast, I couldn't defend myself.

'You've brought shame to this home, you cunt!'

'You're not getting away with it this time.'

'You worthless piece of shit!'

'Disrespecting the Church! Our home!'

Breathing heavily, Bill Starling exhausted himself as I lay on the ground in agony. He'd beaten me good and proper. He picked me up by the hair and kicked me away from him.

I limped to the bathroom to try to clean up the blood. As I looked in the mirror, I started to cry. I hated this life. I hated this man I was forced to call Uncle. I hated everything. I washed the blood off my face, wincing as the cold water stung my skin. Just then Auntie Coral caught sight of me as she passed the bathroom.

'What's your face streaming for?' she snapped. 'Well, you got what you deserved, whatever it was you did.'

We were never allowed back to church after that. Although we didn't care. After all, what had the Catholic Church ever done for us? Nothing.

*

Sometime later, it was my turn again to have to fend off another attempt to sexually abuse me. I'd already escaped the Snatch Squads a few times by now; each time I put up such a fight it wasn't worth it for them. That's the thing about bullies: they're cowards. Why choose to wrestle with a boy with a knife when you can pick on some kid who's already broken?

The staff all had their own techniques for abusing kids, and persuading a kid to 'allow' you to abuse them was one. This was Haydn Davies' preferred method. I'd heard from the older lads how he liked to bugger boys. A couple of them went willingly into his room, while others came out quiet and withdrawn.

'He takes you to his sofa to let you look at porn and then flips you around and fucks you up the arse,' one kid told me. I still didn't know what that meant and I definitely hadn't seen porn before. But when Haydn asked me to come and see him in his staff quarters I was prepared for the worst.

'Come and sit with me, Paul,' he said. Just as I was about to sit down on his sofa, he lifted it up and I saw a big pile of magazines.

He pulled one out and then closed the sofa.

'Come and make yourself comfy, Paul,' he said, opening the magazine. 'Have a good look at these lovely girls.'

He watched my face carefully as I eyed the photos. There were naked ladies with hairy bits and boobs. I'd never seen such things before and was fascinated. Already I could feel stirrings in my trousers as I flicked through the pages. The ladies were all in different positions and wearing fancy knickers.

Cor, I thought. I was, after all, a red-blooded kid.

'Do you like these photos, Paul? Nice, aren't they? You like pretty ladies, I can tell. A good-looking boy like you must do.'

He started to smile and I felt him slide across the sofa, his leg pressed up against mine. Despite the pictures, I edged away. Then he reached out to touch my thigh, before his hand crept up to my groin. I froze for a second and then leapt up as if he'd burned me.

'Nah,' I cried. 'You're not fucking doing nothing!'

I was over by the door before he could react, wrenching it open. To my surprise and relief it wasn't locked.

'Hey, what's wrong?' he asked, trying to sound innocent. He made me feel sick and I was desperate to get away. The other boys had been right. Before he had time to persuade me otherwise, I was out of the door and running down the corridor.

I'd never doubted the stories of the other lads, but now I knew they were right and I felt sickened, my heart beating like a drum.

I returned to the dormitory exhausted, angry and uptight. There was no escape, and I never knew what was going to happen next. Although I had fended off Haydn's advances, I didn't know when the next one would come, and would something happen to stop me being able to protect myself? How could I trust anyone now? He'd been nice to me, I'd almost let my guard down and then he'd tried to assault me. This was a nightmare that wasn't going to end.

*

By the time I'd been at St Leonard's for a couple of years, I was no longer the same little boy who'd arrived from St Vincent's. I'd gone from being a quiet little kid to a very troubled, violent boy with a hair-trigger temper. I picked fights wherever I could, shrugging off pain and injury as if they were nothing. I always fought with the older kids, especially those who tried to pick on the little ones. It was like if I could take some bullies down that made life better somehow, especially as so many adults were bullying us too.

At the age of eleven, the box-ticking by the authorities continued and this time it was the school's turn. Despite neither myself nor Liam being able to read or write, we were made to take the eleven-plus exam. We had to sit down at a desk with a paper and pencil for two hours, even though we could only write our names. Then, as if we had filled them out, the papers were collected and sent off for marking. It was a total farce. Anyway, our future schooling hinged on this eleven-plus. If we passed it, we'd go to the posh grammar school, Campion, in Hornchurch. If we failed, it would be Bishop Ward Catholic School in Dagenham, where all the thick kids who were never going to do anything in life ended up. No prizes for guessing where we were going.

Starting a new school meant we were going to face more bullying, as kids in care were such an easy target. So Liam and I decided we'd face up to the tough nuts, so everyone knew to leave us alone. I took my knife everywhere with me and school would be no exception – in fact, it was needed more than ever until I could suss it out.

We were given the bus fare to go to school with but, realising we could save it for food, we walked the five miles from Hornchurch to Dagenham every day. Our bellies constantly ached with hunger, so we'd buy a chocolate bar or sweets on the way. By now I knew the staff stole most of the food budget for the home, keeping it for themselves. So we lived off small plates of Spam fritters, beans, stale bread and sandwiches. There was never, ever enough. On Saturdays they wheeled out a tray of cheese or ham sandwiches, made with the cheapest supermarket brands of course, and left it in the day room for us to fight over. The big kids always reached it first, kicking away the smaller ones. We fell on any food like animals, eating so fast we'd feel sick. Spare bus fare was like gold dust, so we could buy something, usually cheap carbs like chips or sweets, to make us feel full for a few hours.

Just as we expected, if we'd thought our primary school life was shit, Bishop Ward was hell on earth. The teachers were even meaner and more violent to us than the last lot. So we quickly switched off and spent every lesson messing around or bunking off. Often we'd get the cane before the school day had even begun, as we were late. Teachers caned kids at the drop of a hat in those days and bullying was rife, even from the supposed grownups in charge. My reaction to all of this, aside from sticking with Liam and being a hard nut, was to pretend to have lots of self-confidence. Around this time, I got my new nickname, Jacko. To overcompensate for being the poor kid from the home, I often bowled around the school pretending I was all that.

'You think you're Jack the Lad or something,' shouted one boy during a game of football. And it set off the name *Jack the Lad*, which got shortened to just *Jacko*.

Although all the kids constantly ribbed Liam and me for having shit haircuts or for wearing the cheapest quality uniform, some of the kids were okay. I even found myself getting along with one boy called Andrew, who was from the posh neighbourhood. One afternoon he asked if I wanted to go for tea at his house after school. This had never happened before.

'You sure?' I said, wondering if he'd made a mistake. I was so surprised as us kids from the home never got to mix with the normal kids with parents outside of school.

'Yeah, Mum says it's nice I've made a new friend,' he said.

I was so used to rejection, this felt amazing. I didn't think St Leonard's would allow it, but they did, so the next Thursday I left the school gates with Andrew instead of Liam. We walked through a few nice streets before arriving at a lovely brick-built house on a clean tree-lined avenue. He opened his own door with a key and wiped his feet on the mat by the door, so I copied him.

Being inside his house was like visiting a palace for the first time. I couldn't believe how soft the carpets were, how comfy the sofas were. The walls had framed pictures, not just photos of the family but nice paintings of things like bouquets of flowers and boats. There was a hostess trolley with a tin marked 'Biscuits' on it and wooden cabinets with books on top. It was warm and cosy, words not in my vocabulary. I went to use the loo and upstairs in the bathroom the sheets of bog roll were soft, not like our tracing paper, and the soap smelt nice. The only home I'd ever been in like this was Mary's.

Then, when his mum came home, she said hello and actually hugged Andrew. I didn't know where to look as she swept her arms around him, planting a kiss on his head. I was embarrassed, but envious too. The longing for someone to care for me like that was physically painful.

Before dinnertime we messed around, listening to music in his room and chatting, but smells of cooking meat and potatoes were already sending me crackers. I was so hungry I could have eaten the nice duvet we sat on, and a duvet like his was something I'd never even seen before.

Finally, Andrew's mum called us down and we were seated at the dining table. I was itching to start eating. His dad had just come home from work and he spoke to Andrew nicely too, interested about how his day went. I couldn't believe how nice these people were. Was this what all mums and dads were like? I thought of Auntie Coral's words:

'If you were normal, you would have a mum and dad who loves you. But you're not normal and that's why nobody does!'

When his dad asked me how I was, I stuttered while speaking as nobody had asked me that before. Plus the anticipation of the food arriving was unbearable now. I couldn't even think straight as I knew it was on its way. Then Andrew's mum brought the steaming plates through and my eyes nearly fell out of my head.

There was a glistening slab of steak. Thick, crispy chips. Prawn cocktail! I hadn't ever tried a prawn before. Andrew had barely finished speaking to his dad before I fell on this food like a wolf. Mouthful after mouthful, I barely chewed before swallowing. Head down, I gobbled as fast as I possibly could. I barely looked up to see what anyone else was doing and I didn't want to waste time on conversation now.

'Paul is it?' Andrew's dad asked. I nodded, unable to speak with a mouth full like a hamster's.

I kept shovelling the chips in, barely able to swallow them before cramming in the next one. It tasted so good, it made me giddy. *Imagine,* I thought, looking at Andrew as he politely cut his steak slowly, *you get to come home and eat this every single night!*

I carried on gulping down the dinner in silence, barely noticing Andrew's mum and dad's anxious glances. When I finally finished, I sat back feeling sick, holding my gut like King Henry the Eighth. To feel this full up was such a novelty. When Andrew's mum asked if I'd like seconds, I couldn't believe my luck.

Half an hour later, after I'd demolished a plateful of Black Forest gateau (I didn't have a clue where the Black Forest was, but they made fucking good cakes), the plates were cleared away and it was soon time for me to walk back to St Leonard's. Not surprisingly I wasn't ever asked back to Andrew's. Our friendship soon fizzled out too. After all, what parent wants the troubled kid with no manners to tea? I never went to tea again with anyone from school.

That glimpse into how 'normal' families lived made me feel worse than ever. I'd seen families on the telly before, but I assumed *The Waltons* and Disney movies showed fantasy homes that weren't real. A nice mum and dad. A lovely house with lovely things and good food every day. It was the stuff of dreams… and yet now I knew the truth. Not only was Mary's house like that, but ordinary kids like Andrew had parents and a house like that too. Now when Auntie Coral taunted me about not deserving a real family, which she did every single day, it hurt more than ever. Knowing what you're missing out on makes it worse.

'Remember, if you were normal you wouldn't be here. So shut up, you little cunt,' was one of her favourite sayings. Her voice would echo around my head all day long.

'If you were normal, if you were normal…'

Chapter 5: True Blood

Kids in care have no background, no culture, nothing to cling on to. Teachers at school weren't interested in our wellbeing and neither were our supposed carers. It felt like every grownup we were around played the same broken record to us:

'You're like shit on our shoe.'

So by secondary school my life felt worthless. Instead of wanting to learn, I wanted to fight. Not least of all because that's what adults all around us were teaching us to do. I experienced violence from teachers almost on a daily basis, either because I was late or because I was in fights with other kids. The Paul I had created was becoming stronger and more violent.

One morning my head throbbed so much with hunger I laid my forehead on my arms as my maths lesson began.

'Connolly, raise your head. Now!' yelled my teacher.

I glanced up. This particular morning my vision was especially bad and I felt sick. Most likely I had a migraine through lack of food.

'I said: Head. Up!' he repeated, pointing his stick of chalk at me.

Another few seconds and I knew he'd probably hit me, so I raised my head a bit further, squinting at him. With a look of rage he raced towards me, grabbing a fistful of plastic rules off his desk as he passed by. Then, before I had time to react, he whacked them on the top of my head. I clutched my hair as the whole room seemed to spin. Then I fell off my chair and ran out of the class, trying not to cry.

I hate this place, I thought. *As much as I hate St Leonard's.*

This teacher wasn't the only violent one either. There were many very violent teachers who took great joy in beating kids for petty reasons. One of them was called Mr Singh, a big, fat Indian man who taught metalwork. He'd pace the corridor, cane in his hand, whacking kids for whatever reason he thought of. Others would cane your hand, but accidentally hit your wrists, which hurt even more.

Because we were from the home, older kids liked to pick on us whenever they could. Liam and I stuck together, but we also teamed up with another Irish kid from the home called Justin. We make sure we never walked anywhere alone, because the older ones would come for us.

'You Irish bastards. Got no mum? Got no dad? Aww, who's gonna help you now?' they'd scream at us, given half the chance.

Liam's technique was never to give them half a chance. He'd go for the kids, however big they were, fighting with such ferocity, I always knew he'd win. I started to copy the look of rage on his face to scare them off too.

I was on guard all the time and stuck close to the boys who became like brothers to me, including Lawrence, Michael and Liam. I also met Liam's brother, Seamus. I wasn't close to him, but he seemed like a decent sort, as did all his brothers. Only the St Leonard's boys understood me. As far as I was concerned, the rest of the world could go to hell. This meant I decided to turn my back on Mary too. Her cosy world and nice house had been an anchor for me. But now I felt I didn't belong there, especially as she had a son of her own now. So after that summer, I didn't go back. I never explained how I felt; I just cut her off and stopped answering her calls. She still wrote me letters, which I couldn't read, so I always asked someone else to do it for me. She wanted to know how I was, but even then I never replied. I couldn't see the point. My life was going down a very different road to hers. I couldn't believe she'd want me in it.

As if to hammer home my lack of love, Starling suddenly approached me one day and asked to speak to me in his office.

'We all have mothers, even you, you little cunt, so you're going with your brothers to see your mother.'

That was it, until I saw Declan and John approach me in the courtyard.

'You're coming with us to see our mum,' Declan said. 'It's okay, the old girl gives you money and shit.' I didn't know what to say, so I just agreed. If anything I was curious to meet this woman who was supposed to be my mum.

By now I had learned to keep away from my other brother, Danny, wherever possible. He clearly had it in for me. Perhaps he was jealous of me in some way, but he took every opportunity to remind me who was boss. One morning I was in the day room watching TV when he came in and asked me to turn it over. 'No!' I said. 'That's not fair.' He gave me a hard wallop around the head, knocking me off my chair, and then beat me up while staff looked on. Declan and John seemed okay, not that I had much to do with them. So I couldn't say I was excited at the idea of hanging out with my brothers.

As for my birth mother, she was the strange woman who only turned up for the odd visit and never showed any affection or even made any kind of acknowledgement that I was her boy. I felt nothing for her. Still, I was a little curious as to what this woman who gave birth to me was really like. Desperate for money and food, I decided to go.

I was taken in a taxi with one of the staff to where she lived in Clapton, North London. By the time I got there I was tired and hungry, as usual. We arrived at a rundown house with a Ford Capri parked in the driveway and my brothers were waiting for me outside. The door opened and a woman looked at us. My first thought was how beautiful she was. She had thick auburn hair that reached her shoulders and a pretty face. She wore tight-fitting clothes and looked younger than I'd imagined. She never said hello to any of us, just nodded, and then looked up and down the street before ushering us into the living room, where a big, muscly man was sitting on the sofa.

'Alright, lads,' he said in an Irish accent. I didn't like the look of him, so I quickly sat on the sofa in between my brothers.

Then my birth mum put a plate of biscuits on the table and the others grabbed handfuls of them, leaving just a broken one, so I ate that. I had hoped we'd get more food than this. I was sure that was one point of this visit. She sat opposite me, smoking, not saying anything as she pulled out a purse. She gave us six pence each. Then she looked at me.

'You Paul?' she asked.

'Yeah,' I began.

'Ah, make yourself useful and go across the road and get us twenty Players Number Six, king size, will ya?'

I nodded as she handed me the money. Then she opened the front door, looking anxiously out into the street again.

'I want that change, mind,' she smirked. But as I walked into the road, I'd completely forgotten the brand of cigarettes she'd asked for.

'What was it you wanted again, Mum?' I said loudly before she slammed the front door.

Saying 'Mum' felt weird as I'd never used that word before. I've not used it since either. I either don't use her name or I call her my biological mum (although when I was younger I always referred to her as The Cunt I Came Out Of, however awful that sounds). The irony is that my biological mother's real name is Mary. But she couldn't have been more opposite to the other Mary in my life.

Turns out, however, she didn't like the idea of being called Mum either, because her face twisted into something else after the word left my lips. Reaching for me, she grabbed my collar and pulled me to her face.

'Don't ever call me Mum again. I don't want the neighbours hearing. Do you understand?' she screamed at me.

Shaken, I nodded. I ran to the shop and back, heart racing. All the way I could still feel her hands twisting at the collar of my T-shirt. Why had she been so angry? What had I done? Was calling my own mum 'Mum' so bad? I bought her fags, then ran back to her house, hoping she wouldn't lose it again. As I handed her the fags she barely looked at me, while my brothers talked amongst themselves. Then she lit one and went into the kitchen to make tea, not offering us another cup. I don't remember much conversation, just small talk really. Then it was time to go, so she double-checked the neighbours weren't looking again and said bye. This time I remembered not to use her name; I didn't call her anything.

All the way home my brothers talked about football and girls, not mentioning the visit or how they felt about anything. It was like nothing had happened.

Back at the home, Liam asked where I'd been that day.

'To see my mum,' I said.

His eyebrows shot up and he looked impressed.

'You have a mum? You never said you had a mum. What's this about?'

I shook my head and walked off then. I didn't want to talk about it. He followed me but dropped the subject.

'Want to go and nick some milk?' he asked.

'Yeah, go on then.'

He knew better than to ask questions – we all did. All of this stuff was too painful. We couldn't do fuck all about our situation, so why talk about it?

That night I couldn't sleep. When I did drop off, clutching my knife, I had a dream. There was a lady, who looked like my mum, having babies. She had baby, after baby, after baby. But as each one popped out, she threw it away from her like a rugby ball. No need to be a dream expert to work that one out.

On a handful of occasions I joined my brothers to visit my dad too. Now as odd as this might sound, I don't recall a single conversation I had with him. Again, I went with my brothers to a house in London. They knew him growing up, so had more of a relationship with him. All I recall is an overweight, bald, genial man, wearing a trilby hat, who was into his allotments and gardening. I'd awkwardly sit in his front room, watching my brothers chat to him, until it was time to go home. I don't remember him showing any genuine interest in me or where we were living. Then, he met a new girlfriend called Betty and he moved away and we lost touch. I don't know why, especially as Mary told me he'd tried to keep the family together. Who knows? Maybe he just gave up. I'll never know and can only guess.

Later on I was to meet my sister, Anne, as well. She lived near my birth mum and was fourteen years older than me. She seemed quite kind and treated me in a maternal way, but we didn't have long together.

Basically, my whole family was a bunch of strangers and I was quickly learning that blood is not thicker than water. In the years to come, I simply described myself as an orphan if anyone asked about my family.

*

On the way to school every day, we passed a boathouse next to a lake in a park with a sign that said: *ABC*. We couldn't read, but knew they were the first letters of the alphabet.

'Whaddya think ABC stands for?' I asked Liam one day.

'Dunno,' he said.

Sometimes we saw lorries coming and going. Other times we saw older kids in tracksuits jogging around the lake or men in heavy coats hanging about smoking outside.

But we always noticed the sign, and one day I said, 'Why don't we bunk off and go in?'

'Nah, there's no kids, Jacko,' replied Liam, eyeing the guys hanging around a lorry. 'They might beat us up or something.'

But each time we walked past we always wondered, until one day we dared each other to go in – neither knowing what a huge impact it would have on our lives, or that it was a decision that would one day save my life.

'C'mon,' said Liam. 'Let's go and see this time.'

We wandered down and saw a bloke eyeballing us.

'Ah, let's leave it,' I said, but Liam, always the braver one, stopped me.

'Nah, look we could easily outrun that old cunt. He'll never catch us.'

We walked a bit closer until the bloke was about twenty feet away. He looked hard, with a big, squashed nose and ears that said he'd been in a few fights.

'Alright, boys,' he said. 'Bunking off school, are we?'

'Yeah,' said Liam, not moving any closer.

'Come here, I won't bite ya. You interested in boxing?'

I had no interest, but I could tell Liam's ears had pricked up. He glanced at me and I looked at him.

'Fucking boxing? I'll have a bit of that,' he smiled.

Then another two geezers appeared and we got a bit windy. They all looked like hard nuts. I was about to tug Liam's sleeve to back away when a blond lady appeared and we relaxed a bit. She was gorgeous, with a big chest and red lipstick.

'Hello, boys. You coming in or what?' she asked.

We looked at each other as the blokes nodded.

'Come on, lads. I'll show you around. You can have a go on the bags.'

The guy's name was Alan Mayhew and the lady was his wife, Cathy. The other fellas were Lenny Wilson and Tommy Butler. They showed us around the building. It smelt of sweat and Vicks. There were lots of punch bags hanging up, and a proper boxing ring and a locker room. I spied posters showing boxers who'd fought at the club and also photos of Henry Cooper and Joe Bugner, proper fighters I'd seen on the telly before. Training started at five p.m. and they said if we ever wanted to join in, we were welcome.

'How old are you two?' Alan asked.

'Eleven,' said Liam.

'Fucking hell. I thought you were about seven years old. The size of the pair of you skinny things. Here, Cathy, get these two something to eat, will ya?'

Cathy went and brought us some cheese sandwiches and we ate them in just a few bites.

'Easy!' she said. 'You'll choke.'

She waited until we'd finished before asking more questions.

'You from round here then?' Cathy asked.

'St Leonard's,' said Liam.

Cathy's eyebrows shot up and she glanced at Alan. 'Oh lads… Well, listen. If you ever want to come back, you'll always be welcome. Do come in and say hello, come and see us. Start training whenever you want to.'

'Yeah, too right,' added Alan. 'The door is always open, and we can train you up any time. Tell you what, after school is a good time. Before the senior classes start…'

Both of us looked at each other. Usually when we said we were from the kids' home, people turned their noses up. But instead, since we'd mentioned St Leonard's these people were being even nicer to us.

'We will,' we promised and meant it.

All the way home we didn't stop talking about ABC, which stood for Amateur Boxing Club. To us, it seemed unbelievable that some adults had been kind and even appeared to like us, let alone want to spend time with us.

'We gotta go back, Jacko,' said Liam.

'We definitely do,' I agreed.

The very next day we were back there and we got the same welcome. Cathy brought us a big plate of pork pies and we wolfed it down. We found out Tommy Butler was an Olympic coach, and Alan showed us how to wrap up our hands to put gloves on. We did a few circuits before it was time to leave.

'Come again!' they all said.

Before we left, Cathy pulled us to her and ruffled both our heads. Liam tried to dodge her – he was unable to deal with the show of affection – but I grinned. She looked at us with such affection in her eyes; it felt wonderful to experience this.

'Do you fancy Cathy?' Liam asked as we left.

'Yeah, she's okay,' I said, feeling myself go red. It was true, she was a gorgeous lady.

'But she's like your mum too,' he laughed. 'Cuddling ya like that.'

'Shut up!'

'Ha ha, you want to fuck your mum,' he laughed.

'Fuck off, you cunt!' I cried.

I punched his arm and ran off. He soon caught up. I knew he was only teasing me but it could hurt sometimes.

Every single day now we couldn't wait for school to be over, just so we could visit Dagenham Boxing Club. Those adults were like gods to us already, for one reason and one reason only: they'd showed us kindness. For the first time in our lives we felt wanted, and they didn't have a sexual agenda either. Sounds strange, but if you have never, ever experienced such kindness, you fall in love with whoever offers it to you first.

Because we were committed to the sessions, Alan always spent ages with us. Teaching us, training us. He taught us that boxing is about discipline, focus and looking after yourself. All these things appealed, as he made us feel good. Simple as that.

Little did we know it, but boxing was set to save me. It made me turn away from the drink and drugs that a lot of the other kids got into. It was a long time before we had our first fight, though. This was because we were so small. Liam was much bigger than me, but even he didn't fit into the weight category for kids our own age. Being half-starved meant we'd have to wait to fight kids our age. But just a few months later, we were ready to do gym shows. These were controlled fights in the club with one-minute rounds as a way of coaxing kids into fighting and building confidence. I won all three of mine – the first time I'd ever been good at anything, let alone been praised by adults. It was a revelation and something that changed my life.

*

To avoid both the classrooms and our cottages we spent as long as possible wandering the fields and the streets, bunking off or trying to work out ways to earn some money, or going to the boxing gym. One day, on one of our jaunts to The Chase, we bumped into two middle-aged men in boiler suits near one of the nearby factories. Their names were Bill and Ted (yes, really!) and they worked as sheet- metal workers.

'Here, lads, if you want to earn yourself some pocket money, you can sweep up for us at the end of the day if you like,' one said.

We gladly did the job and were thrilled to get a few pennies at the end of each day. They were nice guys, so we returned there often. Seeing how thin we were, they brought in extra sandwiches in their lunchboxes too.

Often we'd drop in on the horses afterwards. Several times now we'd got to know some of the animals only for them to disappear one day, never to be seen again. Sometimes we'd hear chainsaws being used in the slaughterhouse and feared the worst.

Then one day Liam came up with another one of his bright ideas.

'Hey, Jacko! Let's save the next lot of horses that arrive in the field,' he said.

I laughed. How we would manage this I had no idea, but I always went along with Liam's crazy schemes.

'Yeah, alright,' I said. 'It's worth a try.'

The next week there were new horses in the field and they were so friendly to us, we fell in love with them.

'Right, let's rescue these,' Liam announced.

He jumped on the back of one and I mounted the other. We'd become pretty good riders by now. We walked them down to the river, going further than we'd ever gone before. The horses hesitated a little, but Liam coaxed his on and mine followed.

The water grew deeper and deeper, until the horses had to start swimming. Liam turned to look at me, his eyes shining as he clung to the mane. I copied him, feeling amazed we weren't tumbling off. But the horses seemed to tread carefully as if to make sure we stayed on.

'I trust mine,' said Liam. 'Do you, Jacko?'

'Yeah, I do,' I whispered. It felt wonderful, knowing these beasts were never going to harm us.

We splashed slowly to the other side and Liam jumped down. He'd spotted some old rope to wrap around the horses' noses.

'C'mon, let's lead them away from here. Somewhere safe,' he said.

We started walking down the country lane that led out into the town in Romford, but pretty quickly we were gaining unwanted attention. Drivers started beeping us and old ladies were doing double-takes.

'Where you taking them horses?' someone shouted.

Liam told them to fuck off and I wanted the ground to open up and swallow me.

'Liam,' I hissed. 'We're supposed to be keeping a low profile, bunking off. Not drawing attention to ourselves.'

Our sense of direction was shit. Instead of heading into the Essex countryside we ended up heading into Romford, on market day. By the time we'd reached the town centre, it was obvious this rescue plan wasn't going to work. We'd hoped to stumble across a quiet stable; somewhere we could secretly look after our four-legged friends. Instead, all around were car parks and shops. Our plan had been crazy.

'This ain't gonna work, Liam,' I said.

'Yeah, I know that – shut up, Jacko,' he replied.

We had no choice but to lead the horses back to their field, to await a certain death. We walked back in silence, both gutted we couldn't do anything. As we led them through the gate and untied the rope, they looked us in the eye. Liam pushed his face against his one's nose and the horse seemed to push it back. I noticed tears in Liam's eyes but never dared say anything. I was too busy blinking mine away anyway.

Soon after, Liam found a cat near the home that popped into the playing fields every now and again. He began saving a little milk from his morning cereal for it, sneaking a saucer out when staff weren't looking. This seemed to fulfil his need to care for something and he always talked to me about his cat, but nobody else.

*

Liam always had a new plan up his sleeve. This time it was to make money. We were wandering around Romford market when he stopped in the street, whacking me on the chest with the back of his hand.

'Oi, Paul. I know what we need to do!'

He started running so fast I could barely keep up.

'What the fuck's going on now?'

'Follow me!'

'I'm trying!'

We reached the Debenhams store, where Liam started picking up Parker pens.

'What do you want one of those for?' I asked as he winked at me.

'We're gonna nick them. Nick a load of stuff and sell it on the market,' he said.

'Shhh, will ya,' I replied, eyeing the security guard.

'Nah, I could take him on. Beat him up within fucking seconds or outrun him. Fucking kill him if I wanted to,' he grinned. This was Liam all over, taking stuff to the extreme. But his idea was a good one. It just needed more careful planning.

So instead of just scooping up a load of goods and scarpering, I made a few suggestions so his plan would work.

'Let's put small stuff up our sleeves, like tie pins, pens, purses, easy stuff to hide,' I said. 'We'll get away with that.'

We returned the next day to start at the top of Debenhams. Very swiftly we scooped up loads of small items, from Parker pens to lighters, working floor by floor. Then we ran outside of the Romford centre into the market and put together two old crates and a piece of board we'd borrowed from nearby traders. We laid out our goods and Liam cried out, 'Parker pens for three paahnds!' to attract attention. Within about twenty minutes our stall was surrounded.

'Hey, this is usually a tenner in Debenhams,' said one lady, holding up a pen.

'It's yours for just three quid, Missus,' I winked.

Half an hour later we had sold our stock and had fifty pounds in our pockets, a huge sum for us kids. Neither of us needed to ask what we wanted to spend it on. We ran into the nearest Wimpy and ordered everything off the menu. Then we sat and stuffed ourselves until we wanted to be sick.

Afterwards we went to a supermarket and bought bread, cakes and anything else we could carry.

'Where are we gonna stash this?' I asked Liam. If the staff caught us, they would confiscate it. Any extras were not allowed in the home, unless parents or a relative brought them in, and even then Bill Starling often confiscated them.

We sneaked up the drive of St Leonard's and quickly dug a hole with our hands underneath a bush before burying our stash like squirrels. Liam looked at me, pleased as punch.

'We won't be fucking hungry after breakfast now, Jacko,' he said.

That night when I waved goodnight to him from my cottage window I imagined his grin was even wider than usual.

'Night, Jacko,' he mouthed.

'Night-night, Liam,' I whispered.

Chapter 6: On the Ropes

Once a month or so, we did the same thing: looted floors in Debenhams and then set up a temporary stall to flog our stolen stash. Afterwards, we'd spend our money straight away on any food we could lay our hands on. KFC was a favourite. Pulling that soft, chewy coating off and sinking our teeth into tasty meat on the bone was like dying and going to heaven, since we got nothing but overcooked Spam at the home. (Little did we know it then but the staff were actually stealing our food budget for themselves. Uncle Bill had a metal box room that was supposed to be used as a safe room for staff in case everything kicked off with the kids, but instead was full of nice food for them and the kids they favoured for sexual abuse.) Finding a way to feed ourselves was like winning the lottery ten times over.

Bunking off school to earn money or visit the horses or train at the gym became the norm. Nobody seemed to notice we were missing from school. Until one day they did, and Bill Starling got wind of it. I had no idea what had happened until I felt a pair of hairy hands grab me from behind a door. It was Uncle Bill, who'd been waiting to pounce.

'C'mere, you little cunt!' he screamed.

He punched me with full force in the face, then spun me around and marched me up the stairs.

'Who's the little smart arse now then?' he spat.

One of his favourite ways to inflict pain on kids was to punch them up the stairs one by one and then kick them down again. Today it was my turn to have the technique used on me.

'Think you can get away with it, do you? Bunking off school? Think I wouldn't find out, eh?' he screamed between blows.

My face was a mess of blood as I struggled to avoid his next strike, but I couldn't because he was so much stronger than me. He was a thickset grown man and I was an undernourished kid, so I stood no chance. Then he slammed me against the wall so hard I felt all my bones rattle. I tried to stand up again, but his rage was relentless.

'You snivelling, worthless shite,' he half-laughed.

Next he picked me up and pushed me over the banister, so I fell down three flights of stairs into the stairwell below.

I had no time to react or yell before I landed in a heap, half on a sofa sticking out from a cubby hole under the stairs. For a while, everything went dark and silent. Then I opened my eyes to see some kids standing over me, poking my arm. I hadn't a clue what had happened for a minute, feeling nothing but intense pain in my ribs. I tried to sit up but couldn't, so a couple of the kids half-carried me to the sick bay. It was agony just trying to breathe in. There, a nurse from St Leonard's looked me over.

'Ooh, you've broken some ribs,' she said. 'Not much we can do about that, so just lie down for now.'

I was put in a bed for the night, next to a kid with measles. Hours later the lights went out, but the pain was so bad I could barely sleep.

The next morning, determined to try to get up, I lifted my legs over the side of the bed, but collapsed. My own legs couldn't take my body weight! Panicking, I turned back to climb onto the bed. This had never happened to me before and I felt so scared. Maybe I was really hurt and was gonna die all alone in this bed?

I waited for a few hours and tried again, and this time thankfully I could stand, although I wobbled like Bambi. A day later I was back in my cottage, keen to hide my pain from the others. I didn't want to seem weak. Auntie Coral noticed me wincing, however. She never missed a beat, that one.

'Got a good hiding did you, Paul? Well, you know you deserved it. Fact is, if you were loved and normal, you wouldn't even be here, would you? So no point in snivelling about it, eh?' she smirked.

Looking back, I realise Bill could have killed me that day. He had no way of knowing if I would survive that fall, down three flights. It was an impulsive move he made to teach me a lesson. Since then I have heard of kids who did die in the home, but with nobody checking up on their welfare, no parents to quiz authorities, deaths were written off as suicides. Kids regularly used to smoke in the loft and I heard of one who burned to death, and another who was found dead in a bedroom. When nobody cares about kids, nobody asks questions.

Two days later, I saw Liam and told him what had happened as we walked to school.

'He's a fucking bastard,' he said. 'One day I am going fucking kill them all. Pop their eyes out of their heads, the dirty cunts. Slit their throats…'

We went into a fantasy world about what we could do to them, especially with our newfound boxing skills. Thank God we were learning to be proper fighters!

'One day, Liam,' I agreed. 'One day…'

*

By now Uncle Bill and Auntie Coral had discovered we were going to boxing after school most nights, because we were getting back later than other kids. Predictably, they didn't like the idea.

'You're wasting your time and theirs. As if the likes of you will ever be boxers,' cried Auntie Coral. 'You're just a pair of stupid, worthless bastards who'll never amount to anything. The only place you'll end up is dead or in the nick, mark my words.'

Auntie Coral had told me this pretty much every single day since I'd arrived, but nothing was going to stop me training. The coaches there and Cathy were like angels in comparison to Uncle Bill and Auntie Coral and her evil mouth. So we ignored them and, bar locking us in, they couldn't stop us going.

Besides, boxing had become mine and Liam's favourite thing. We were such a team; we'd never be seen without each other. We rarely argued but often did play-fight together, Liam always dominating me as he was still bigger and more of a street fighter. He never really hurt me, even though he could have. Often he'd end up giving me a hug in between practising our boxing moves. This was a brief moment of love between us. We were so starved of affection, we found it between ourselves. Of course he'd never openly ask for a cuddle and neither would I; we were too laddish for that lark. But those hugs meant a lot to me and I'm sure they did to him.

Our boxing skills gave us even more confidence outside St Leonard's, where the world seemed like an unfriendly jungle. We were the poor kids with shitty, cheap clothes that nobody liked, and given half the chance most kids ribbed us when they could. So it went without saying that we had to stick up for ourselves – and, if we could, other kids who were bullied. After all, if we couldn't stand up to the many bullies at St Leonard's, we could do so outside on the streets.

One afternoon we were in a menswear shop, eyeing up clothes we'd never afford, when a group of boys from the school wandered in. One of them was a black kid.

'How cool is that,' he said, pointing to a parka coat.

Just then three fifteen-year-old lads from school showed up and started teasing him.

'Why's a black fuck like you eyeing up white man's clothes?' one said. They all laughed, shoving the boy in the back.

'What's your fucking problem?' Liam asked. 'He can look if he wants. Leave him alone.'

Neither of us ever missed a beat when it came to a potential punch-up in the air.

The ringleader made a whistling sound and gave the others a sideways glance, as if to say, *Who does he think he is?*

'You want some as well then?' he sneered at Liam. 'St Leonard's scum.'

Just one tiny glance from Liam in my direction told me to go for it. Without warning, we tore into the three of them, punching as hard as we could. Instantly they knew we meant business. I saw the whites of their eyes because they'd totally underestimated us. I knocked one to the floor, while Liam did the others Two of them managed to get up and they ran away like a pair of girls, but Liam had the ringleader on the floor. He was punching him – *whack, whack, whack* – so the skin around his lips and eyes tore open like a watermelon.

'Alright, Liam,' I said, trying to pull him off.

But Liam continued, pummelling the boy like he might get away. Blood started splattering over the floor.

'He's going nowhere. Leave him!' I cried. But Liam carried on as if I'd said nothing. Panicking he might kill the boy, I started wrenching Liam's blazer.

'Leave it!' I had to scream before he finally stopped.

We both ran away as fast as we could; only stopping on a side street to catch our breath.

'You coulda killed him,' I gasped, trying to catch Liam's eye.

He looked calmer now and grinned. 'And so what if I had?' he laughed. 'Serves them fucking right for thinking we were just a pair of cunts who can't handle ourselves.'

This was Liam all over. He had that much rage inside. As crazy as it was to watch sometimes, I understood this. After my time at St Leonard's, I had the same bubbling rage deep within me. We walked happily off to our boxing session, pleased we'd seen off the bullies.

We never missed a training session, and Liam became known as my shadow as one of us was never seen without the other. We loved the circuits, seeing our bodies growing stronger and stronger, taught by men we trusted. Lenny even taught us moves like jumping on our tensed stomachs without us flinching. For a pair of boys who'd only ever been hit by adult men, this was a big leap of faith. Little did we know that our love of boxing would come to test our loyalty though.

*

As the months passed, Alan saw potential in me and Tommy, the coach, started doing one-to-one sessions. They were teaching Liam and me everything they knew about boxing, but also how it related to street fighting. Clever tricks like how to jab left over left and then lead your opponent around to a big right hand. Or throw a shot over your shoulder and elbow them accidentally on purpose. They taught me ring craft, how to use your feet and turn your opponent on the ropes. I had no interest whatsoever in school, but I was desperate to please these men, so I put my all into it and found I was a fast learner. I learned that boxing was about more than just throwing punches and lapped it up. Liam, on the other hand, was a great fighter, but he stuck to the moves he already knew. He was too stubborn and sure of himself to get good at proper techniques, so it meant while I progressed, he carried on brawling.

'Jacko, you're a right fucking brown-noser. You trying to impress Cathy or something?' he jeered at me one session.

He'd picked up on the fact I found her attractive, as did he. We loved her for looking after us, feeding us up whenever she could, but there was no hiding the fact she was beautiful as well.

'Aww, shut up,' I yelled at him. 'You're talking shit, Liam.'

Violence in the ring was controlled, whereas violence out of the ring was based on fear. There was plenty of that at St Leonard's, but even outside the home it seemed to follow us kids from care wherever we went. One day, Tommy Maloney took me to East London to where his family were from. I was terrified of Tommy but also in awe, even if I tried not to show it, so when he suggested I join him, I went. Aged just sixteen, he was already an absolute maniac; an angry, nasty young man who loved a fist fight. He'd return on a Saturday night from punch-ups with grown men in pubs and proudly show off the bruises.

On our trip, he took me to a local greasy spoon cafe in Stepney near where he'd lived. He walked in and ordered food, but then refused to pay for it. He didn't have any money anyway – none of us did.

Fucking hell, I thought as the boss of the cafe just nodded and offered him a seat. *These people totally respect him around here.*

A few people moved as Tommy got served his egg and chips (he let me have a couple too). I noticed customers eyeing him nervously, and a few leaving the cafe altogether. Of course he wasn't respected at all – he'd put the fear of God into people and they wanted to avoid the trouble he brought. But watching this at the age of twelve, I was proper impressed.

Around this time, my brother, John, disappeared from the home and I heard from my social worker unexpectedly.

'He's in Borstal,' she said. 'You need to go and visit him.'

'What did he do?' I asked.

I'd never known anyone go to prison before. I mean, Auntie Coral was always telling me that's where I'd end up, but I'd never actually heard of anyone I knew in the slammer. She didn't explain what John had done, but later on one of the other kids told me he'd been caught mugging old ladies in the street. Bashing them over the head and grabbing their handbag. The idea of him doing this upset me.

How could he? I thought. The idea of hurting old people didn't seem right. Celia Stock didn't ask me if I wanted to visit him. If she had asked, I'd have said no.

So one Saturday morning, instead of disappearing to the playing fields with Liam, I had to go on a train ride to Reading, to St Benedict's Approved School for Roman Catholic Boys. It was run by the Brothers of the Christian School, and boys there would get training in farming and gardening on the sprawling country estate. The idea was to turn troubled lives around, but the brutality I saw there was even beyond what was happening at St Leonard's. When we arrived, Celia said she'd leave me to it.

'Go and say hello to your brother and see how he's doing,' she said. 'I'll catch up with you later.'

Minutes later, John wandered into the room where I was waiting. He nodded and raised his eyebrows as a hello, and then pissed off again. Realising he wasn't the least bit interested in me visiting, I took myself off to the games room to kill time before visiting hours were up.

Inside, boys were playing snooker, but it wasn't long before things turned nasty. One kid pulled off his sock and stuck a ball in it, while the other was armed with a snooker cue. They started fighting viciously, giving everything they had. Before, I'd generally seen fights between boys who were mismatched. There was always a weaker person. But in this case, as they fell to the floor, punching and kicking, they were as ferocious as each other. It was like a scene from the film *Scum* that I watched years later. My heart was racing as I watched, wide-eyed. These boys were smashing the hell out of each other.

Fascinated, but eager to get away, I slipped off and wandered down the corridor into the canteen. Here, kids were lined up with trays, having food slopped onto plates. It looked like a prison.

So this is my next stop, I thought grimly, Auntie Coral's words in my head. She told me on a regularly basis I'd end up dead or in prison. I wondered for the first time if death was preferable to a hellhole like this. I knew I didn't want it to be true, but I assumed, as an adult, she knew more than me about life.

I found a bench to sit on and wait for Celia to find me. Suddenly, an older boy appeared at my side.

'You Paul Connolly?' he said, glaring at me.

I started to nod as he grabbed my hand. He held it in between his two palms and slowly began to bend all my fingers back.

'Owww, owwww,' I cried.

I tried to pull away but his grip was like a vice. He stared me in the eyes, pulling and pulling until I began to cry.

'Arghhh, you're breaking them,' I sobbed.

'Tell your brother, John, I did this,' he spat before letting go. He clearly had a bone to pick with my brother, but why pick on me? I snatched my hand back, my head spinning with pain. I never did tell John, as I didn't think he'd care.

Finally, Celia came to collect me, bright and breezy as always.

'Come on, you,' she said. 'Hope it was nice to see your brother and you enjoyed your visit.' Another box ticked for her today.

Violence had become a massive part of my life now. Not only was I seeing it all around me, learning the craft in the ring, but my fear and anxiety made my temper uncontrollable. After all, this was what I'd been doing for the last few years every day at St Leonard's. It got to the point that my coach, Tommy pulled me aside during a session one weekend. He was a distinguished ex-forces man who even managed to look smart in his immaculate Adidas tracksuit. When he spoke, you listened.

'If you want to win at boxing, you need to clean it up. Nobody will take you seriously if you're disqualified,' Tommy warned me.

Alan was also like a superhero and a demigod all rolled into one. I mean, this was a man who showed us how you could be tough but kind at the same time. He didn't take any crap from anyone, but knew right from wrong. He had manners and loved his wife, Cathy, and his club and his boys. Both Tommy and Alan were like a father to me in different ways.

'Yes, Tommy,' I said, soaking up his words. I meant it too. As dirty as I fought outside the ring, I wanted to be good at this.

Meanwhile, Liam was still struggling, and while I was allowed to fight kids aged sixteen or seventeen while I was only twelve, Liam was still with kids his own age.

My best friend was always stronger than me, but I started to paste him when sparring together too. If we did spar together, often he used dirty tricks of his own to distract me. Once, I was ducking and diving, guessing where he was about to throw another punch, when he suddenly said, 'Hey, your mum is here!' and I turned to see Cathy arriving. Then – *whack* – he had me on the floor. His teasing was getting a bit much, as was his jealousy that I was the boxing golden boy. But I let it go, as Liam was like a proper brother to me – unlike the ones I actually had.

Chapter 7: Fighting Back

By the age of thirteen, I was a mess. My violent streak mixed with hormones was an explosive combination.

Like many of the kids, I'd begun to self-harm. My knife was always in my hand or back pocket, so one day I started to poke myself with it. Then I made a little cut and watched it bleed. *Ooh, that feels weird,* I thought. Then I did another one, and another one. It felt good to be in control of the pain. For once, I was choosing to hurt myself rather than someone doing it to me.

Glue-sniffing also became a big hobby for kids. Mark Byrnes and George loved the stuff. They'd sit under our cottage windowsill, their heads in plastic bags, sucking in-out, in-out like madmen. Then they'd roll around the grass, giggling uncontrollably, high as kites. It was one of the few times you heard genuine laughter at St Leonard's. Other lads tried it too, but I never did. Thankfully, boxing had given me a need to be in control. I understood that glue-sniffing would affect my breathing and make training harder.

We all found our ways to escape. One girl, Jean Worrall, loved attention from boys and would seduce them by lifting up her skirt and letting a queue of lads touch her, poor kid. Lads would rub their privates up against her, laughing and joking while they did it. Looking back, I realise now Jean must have had learning difficulties. Like many kids who had special needs, either from birth or through neglect, nobody recognised this or supported her.

Kids were having sex from a very young age too. Lawrence was one of many boys who lost his virginity at only about eleven or twelve. He really had the gift of the gab when it came to girls and used to persuade local girls to go to the end of our drive and lift their tops up. 'Come on, lads,' he'd say. 'I have a treat in store.' And we'd follow him to find a gang of giggling girls, all happy for us to feel them up for a bit. Despite all of this, I was relatively immature and more interested in boxing gloves than getting into girls' knickers.

St Leonard's had been built in beautiful countryside as a haven for the unwanted kids of East London, but at the weekends those fields were filled with miserable kids trying to find an escape. Self-harm, sexual favours, glue-sniffing, fighting... we were all lost in our own worlds, trying to get away from it all. The unbearable tension, the rejection, the neglect meant unhappiness was everywhere and it was a case of any escape, even for a few minutes, was better than nothing.

One Saturday afternoon, Mark and George were rolling around as usual outside on the playing field with their glue bags, when suddenly there was shouting.

'He can't breathe!' yelled George.

Kids started running towards the sick bay to get staff as Mark lay clutching his throat, making a gurgling sound. An ambulance was called and he was whisked away with an oxygen mask on. As usual, staff were matter-of-fact about it. There were no warnings about the use of solvents, and no sympathy was shown. Mark just came back a few days later and carried on doing it.

The only happy memory of all my time at St Leonard's was being picked to do the Nijmegen four-day march in Holland. Because Liam and I were fit from our boxing, we were picked to go and we couldn't have been happier. Obviously this was the first time I was going abroad; in fact, it was the first time in a while I was leaving Essex. And not only was it a chance to escape for a few days, but our abusers were not coming with us.

'It's fucking brilliant,' Liam grinned.

We started training, walking along the A127 from Hornchurch to Southend every weekend with the other twenty kids chosen to represent our home. The whole march was organised by Datner, an ex-military man who wanted to show off how well we were doing. Trust me not to make things easy, however. About a week before we were due to set off, I had another accident crossing a road. This time I was hit by a bus and landed heavily on my arm, breaking it. This was actually the third time it had happened: once when I was eight, then when I was eleven on the way to school on a crossing and now this. I was taken to hospital on my own, X-rayed and put in a cast, then sent back to the home. As usual, Auntie Coral did nothing but jeer at me.

'Well, well, what a surprise. You're such a stupid, dumb cunt,' she laughed. 'Didn't see it coming, eh? Told you you'll be dead soon after eighteen.'

As much as I hated her, I thought she might be right. By now there were several basic things I didn't know how to do because nobody had ever taught me. As daft as it sounds, I couldn't even piss into a toilet properly. Nobody had ever shown me how to aim or, excuse the graphic image, to pull back my foreskin. It's little things like this that kids in care never find out, as you need someone close to teach you.

I was terrified I wouldn't make the trip to Holland despite having trained for months for it. By now, Datner had left and Alan Prescott had taken over as head of the home, but he didn't care whether I was injured or not, so I was still allowed to go with my broken arm.

The march itself was fun and a break from all the abuse and misery at St Leonard's. We went with different carers who all seemed to quite like us kids. We ended up at the finish line, marching to attention behind the British paratroopers, as the crowds that lined the streets cheered us on. We even saw the Royal Family of the Netherlands, including Princess Laurentian, a beautiful lady who waved to everyone.

'Cor, look at this fucking lot, Liam,' I whispered, waving back at her. Something like this to us boys, who nobody ever noticed, was really special.

Afterwards, Liam and I went off on our own, winding up in Amsterdam's infamous red-light district. Seeing all the birds in their bras and knickers in the windows was an eye-opener to us, and we wandered up and down the narrow streets of Amsterdam with our tongues hanging out. Hours later, staff finally caught up with our mini-trip and brought us back to the hostel where we were staying. It had all been a great adventure, and hundreds of miles away from Bill Starling too.

St Leonard's also made kids take part in the Duke of Edinburgh's Award scheme. The local newspaper even sent a reporter to take photos of kids when they got their medals. 'Youngsters Reach the Heights' the headline read, with a photo of the kids who took part in some expedition smiling proudly and holding certificates.

So to the outside world, everything looked good. Unwanted kids from St Leonard's took part in activities and achieved stuff. Little did anyone know that behind those smiles were kids who were hiding unimaginable traumas.

*

By now there was a new kid in our dorm. Simon was a cool kid I knew not to mess with. He was a good-looking boy, flash, with designer clothes, and always had money on him. He soon ran the card school, where we played for anything from pennies to sweets. He came to live at the home at the age of thirteen, but with his swagger he seemed older and worldlier than all of us. But it soon became clear we weren't his only admirers. I spotted that wherever he went, so did Prescott. Simon used to always have to disappear to Prescott's staff quarters, then he'd return with more money. I began to suspect something was going on. Of course, nobody asked him outright and nothing was said. It was just accepted as a given that Simon had more than us and was one of the favourites.

With Prescott in charge now, the relationships with staff and kids were abusive on so many levels. Not only were some boys and girls being groomed into agreeing to have sex, but as the kids got older they were being seduced into having affairs with staff. Auntie Coral got pregnant by Trevor Philips – a rumour quickly went around after Coral started putting on weight and then it turned into a very obvious baby bump. Philips also had a girlfriend, a pretty black girl called Siobhan, and Coral hated her with a passion. This must have been jealousy. Again, it shows how unhealthy and wrong all the relationships were. Coral went away to have the baby and apparently brought the child up as her own and her husband's.

Meanwhile, Coral had a sister who joined the house as a carer. She was a vile woman too, and was always on at us to get out of bed in the morning for her own sick desires.

'Come on, boys, up you get. I want to see who has the biggest willy,' she'd say, eyeing us up and down. I'd get up and tell her to fuck off, but some boys pulled down their pyjamas to show her. It was all made out to be a big joke by her, but none of us found it funny. I felt violated around her.

Later on I heard that my brother, Peter, had a fling with Coral, but ditched her and treated her badly. He was only thirteen when he first had sex with her and he was 16 by the time it was over. Apparently he used to have sex with her and then laugh about it afterwards, ignoring her. Perhaps this was why she hated me so much? Whatever the reason, it was all so twisted.

There were also very young girls in relationships with older carers – like Peter Setchfield, who was convicted in 2017 of eleven counts of indecently assaulting a young boy and girl under the age of fourteen. He would take them to staff quarters and even drive them to hotels in Kent and Chester to sexually abuse them. One of his victims, a man now in his forties, came forward in 2013. But there were many, many more incidents that never came to court. One girl even moved in with a carer called Ron Wickham, and married him when she was seventeen or eighteen and he was in his fifties. Again, nobody intervened or saw this as odd. I imagine she did it for the security, but what kind of man was he, having sex with a vulnerable young girl in his care? It's disgusting.

There were more boys than girls in the home, so this meant a girl who made herself 'available' was always popular. A terrible thing, but for many kids being touched sexually was the only time anyone showed them any affection. That included staff as well.

Then came a big scandal. Jean Worrall had to have a pregnancy test and the police were called. All the boys at the home were suspected of abuse and some were questioned. The great irony, of course, was that the staff were abusing us and getting away with it, whilst we were under the spotlight when a girl with learning difficulties cried wolf. It turned out to be a false alarm: Jean wasn't pregnant. I doubt anyone actually had sex with her anyway; the poor girl just did it for attention, as it was the only way to get any. Like many kids, she was so starved of any form of physical affection that getting touched up by a group of lads was better than nothing at all.

When it came to abusing kids, all the carers had different tastes and did it differently. Bill Starling preferred to persuade the kids to go along with his abuse. He'd give them extra sweets, food, freedom and money, and they'd go along with it. He'd allow his favourites into his staff quarters, where God knows what was happening to them behind closed doors. He preferred young ones from the age of four.

Haydn Davies, meanwhile, preferred to fuck young boys by showing them porn, getting them aroused and then buggering them.

Alan Prescott always got horny when he was pissed and liked boys who had just begun developing. During the day, he'd shower kids with extra food or fags and then make them sleep with him in the staff quarters. Later on, Setchfield did the same thing.

Then, of course, they all had a go during the Snatch Squads after the pub on a Saturday night, clearly getting off on the violent element. These were paedophiles who were turned on by fear.

Unable to escape all the sexual goings-on, I ended up having a kiss and cuddle with a beautiful girl called Maria. She was mixed-race and I did fancy her. She let me cuddle her one day and I found myself getting a bit too excited and messing my pyjamas before anything else happened. Feeling mortified, I ran away and I decided sex wasn't for me, for a while.

By now I had developed really unhealthy feelings towards women. Basically, with my birth mother and Auntie Coral as my only role models, I thought I hated adult women.

So far I'd escaped two attempts to rape me, the first with the Snatch Squads and the second with Haydn Davies. But next it was Alan Prescott's turn. As his twisted sexual preference was older boys who'd just hit puberty, he waited until I was thirteen.

I was ironing a shirt in the day room one evening when he came in from the pub. As he sidled up to me, I could feel his hard penis on my leg. I spun around. His fat, leering face was in mine, his breath beery and his piercing blue stare on me.

'You're a big boy now, Paul, aren't you?' he said.

Fact was, I was just his type now I'd reached puberty, the age he liked. Plus, I'd been working out at the boxing club, so had muscles. But I'd got this far without being sexually abused, so I wasn't going to take any shit now. I picked up the iron and, for a split second, imagined holding it to his face. But something inside stop me doing it. Instead, I just let rip at him.

'What the fuck are you doing? You fat cunt! Fuck off!' I yelled. I pulled out my trusty knife, which I always carried in my back pocket. He glanced down at it, taken off guard. 'I'll cut your fucking balls off with this,' I spat in his face with fury.

He started walking backwards. I could tell by his face he was scared and that made me feel good as I trembled with rage. So I came towards him, brandishing my knife.

'Fuck off, I said!' I screamed.

I'd lost my temper now and all my self-control with it. I rushed at him and he managed to get behind the door just in time before I sank the tip of my blade into the door.

'Help me keep the door shut,' he yelled at the kids.

I could hear them screaming as they pressed behind it, but I didn't care. All I could see was his fat, horrible face in mine. He had to know never, ever to come near me again, so I started to stab the door, over and over again. Like an automaton, I just went for it. *Stab, stab, stab, stab…*

It felt as if someone had taken over my arm.

Stab, stab, stab…

'I will fucking kill you!' I screamed, my face purple.

I imagined the door was Alan as I carried on stabbing.

'Stay away from me. You do that again and you will DIE!' I continued.

I kept going until my arm ached, then I stopped, knowing there was no way he was going to touch me again.

I stepped backwards, hearing the cries of the kids, my guts twisting a bit at the sound. Taking one last look at the door, the wood now covered with stab marks, I walked away, satisfied he'd never try anything again.

That was the day I realised the tables could turn. I'd finally shown one of the bastards what I was capable of. Protecting myself – and perhaps even, one day, other people. There's no sweeter moment than forcing a bully to reveal what a coward he really is.

Chapter 8: Dare to Dream

I was covered in scars and bruises by now, and the only people who took any notice of them were at boxing. Cathy and Alan often asked if things were okay and Liam and I always said they were. Again, we didn't believe anyone would listen to us even if we trusted them. Besides, what could Cathy and Alan do? If they confronted the staff, we'd only get an even bigger beating afterwards. No, it was easier just to shrug things off and let everyone assume the bruises were just from fights with other kids. Then, one day, something happened that changed everything.

I was in the cold tiled Victorian bathroom getting washed in the bath. There were two baths in the middle of the horrible room, and we only ever had a quick wash as often kids were abused by staff in there. Just as I was getting out to dry myself, Auntie Coral burst in. Like always, there was no respect for privacy or modesty.

'Oi, Paul, you little cunt, clean that bath!' she said, pointing at the bath I hadn't used. She was right, there was soap scum all around the edge, but it wasn't my mess.

'I didn't use that one,' I explained, wrapping the towel around myself. She always made me feel uncomfortable and I was expecting some barbed comments about my dick or body. But instead she seemed to have the hump about cleaning.

'I don't care. I want you to fucking clean it,' she spat.

'I'm not your fucking skivvy,' I said. The older I'd got, the more lippy I'd become, even if it got me into trouble.

Without warning, Bill Starling rushed in. He'd overheard my backchat and loved any excuse to be violent. He grabbed me by the hair, punching me with full force in the face. Then he took me by the scruff of my neck and smashed my head as hard as he could against the frosted glass of the bathroom window. Light splintered in my eyes as I fell backwards. There was no pain, just shock. I clutched my head as I heard him screaming at me.

'Don't speak to your Auntie Coral like that, you fucking scumbag!'

My hands were covered in hot blood and my head was killing me. I heard Auntie Coral saying that I deserved everything I got.

For a few moments I lay there, unable to move and freezing – the towel had dropped off me.

'You little piece of shit,' Starling snarled, standing over me.

At that moment I actually thought: *He's right.* Because lying there, naked and covered in blood, I'd never felt so low and humiliated in my life. Satisfied he'd hurt me enough, he left, and Auntie Coral with him.

I was still dazed when, a few minutes later, I heard voices. We often had kids from outside coming to St Leonard's to do training courses or use our playing fields, and these were teens doing something for St John's Ambulance.

'You okay, mate?' one asked. He helped me sit up, while a couple of them stood there, staring at me.

'What happened?' another said.

'I hurt myself,' I mumbled, knowing there was little point in telling the truth.

'You need to get that seen to,' one said, wrapping my head in a towel. They helped me to my feet and I staggered off to the medical room, where they helped me dress. There, nobody asked me what had happened or how I'd hurt my head. They told me to go to A&E.

'How will I get there?' I asked.

'Bus?' someone suggested.

Still dazed, I looked at my feet as I navigated my way up the driveway with the towel around my head. Only when I jumped on the bus did I realise I didn't have any money.

'Where you going, son?' asked the driver.

'Hospital,' I mumbled, trying to see from under the bloodied towel.

'Don't worry about paying,' he said, eyeing my wound.

I got off at Oldchurch Hospital in Romford and walked into A&E, where doctors stitched me up. They asked me why I was on my own and I just shrugged.

'Someone should see you,' they said and they called social services. Then I was told to go back.

By now it was about three p.m. and school was out, but despite everything I didn't want to miss training. That was our only safe haven. So I got on a bus to go back, but this time I didn't look injured and the driver turfed me off without money for the fare. This left me no choice but to walk the three-mile journey home, so I set off as fast as I could. Exhausted, I arrived at the home to find Liam waiting for me.

'Fucking hell, what happened to you?' he asked, nodding at the stitches.

'Nothing,' I shrugged. 'Come on, let's go to training.'

Clouds were gathering as we set off on the five-mile walk to the club. It soon started raining. Liam was the only one to have a coat and he took it off as he saw me shivering.

'You need this, Paul,' he said, pushing it around my shoulders. Liam knew I'd got hurt, but he respected the fact I didn't want to talk about it, so he didn't pry. I wore the coat until he started shivering and then we kept swapping it.

By the time we arrived, the rain had soaked us both through. We walked in and went straight to the changing rooms. Liam kept looking at me anxiously as he started wrapping up.

'You okay?' he asked.

'Yeah.'

'You sure?'

I shrugged. I sat down for a moment but felt unable to stand again. Every part of my body was aching. Liam went out and returned with Alan.

'Alright, Jacko? Liam said there's been a bit of trouble. Been in a scrap, eh?' Alan asked.

He looked at me, but I couldn't look at him. I didn't want to talk about it. Partly because there was no point and partly through embarrassment.

'Paul?' he said softly.

He reached out to touch me, but I flinched automatically. My head was hurting so bad, I could hardly breathe. He left and then returned with Cathy.

'You okay, Jacko?' she asked. 'Come on. Stand up. Let's have a look at you.'

I hated it, but felt my eyes fill up with tears. Just hearing her soft, concerned voice made me well up.

'What's happened, my darling?' she whispered.

Wincing, I got up, but I couldn't stand straight. It hurt too much. She gasped as she looked at my face. Alan started pacing the room and I sensed he was frustrated. She threw him a look that said, 'Not now', before kneeling down next to me.

'You're safe with us,' she whispered. 'Can I see?'

She started helping me to take my top off and I let her this time. That's when she gasped and pulled me gently to her. I could feel the heat of her on my skin, and for just a few seconds I let myself relax. This cuddle was like being in a warm bath and I longed to stay in her arms. Just to feel safe for once.

'Oh, Paul,' she soothed, stroking my hair.

She was holding back the tears as Alan paced the room.

'Right,' he said. 'It's important you tell us who did this.'

'Tell Alan, sweetie,' she said.

I tried to speak but no words were coming out. I could feel Liam staring, willing me on.

'Bill Starling,' I managed to say. 'At the kids' home. He did it.'

Alan turned and punched the lockers, hitting them so hard the metal doors buckled and it made us all jump.

'Calm down around the kids, for God's sake,' Cathy said.

I gazed at Cathy's blouse, which had turned red with my blood, as Alan turned his back to leave. He yelled the names of some of the men in the gym and everyone left in a commotion as Cathy looked on anxiously.

'We're here for you,' she promised.

Alan didn't come back for a while, so after making us warm, sweet tea and sandwiches, Cathy said we could stay for the night in the gym.

'I don't like sending you back there, but hopefully you'll be safe now,' she said.

I didn't know what she meant, but I was feeling so sleepy now I just wanted to go to bed. Then the next day, we got the bus back to the home and, aching all over, I held on to Liam as we walked down the long driveway by ourselves. But it wasn't long before kids started to crowd around us.

'You'll never guess what happened,' said Mark Byrnes.

'They scared the shit out of Starling. He shit himself,' said Lawrence.

'They had guns and everything,' added Michael.

'They all came in! A whole load of them! In a car!' said Joan Worrall.

We couldn't get a word in edgeways, there was so much excitement. Then, finally, we heard the full story. Alan had rounded up a couple of his mates, driven his car at speed up the home's driveway and demanded to see Bill Starling. They'd run up and down the driveway, looking in cottages and shooting a gun into the sky.

'Where is he?' Alan had yelled.

Terrified, Bill and Coral had run into the metal safe room where they kept food and money and whatever else they stole from us. They'd bolted the door as Alan screamed through the other side for Bill to face him. But like all bullies, Bill Starling was a coward, and he stayed hidden. Not to be beaten, Alan and his men grabbed one of the long dining-room benches we sat on and ran at the metal door with it.

'You won't be locked in that room forever!' cried Alan when the door didn't budge. 'If you ever touch Paul Connolly again, I will come back and blow your fucking head off your shoulders. Got it?'

Then they left. Half an hour later, Starling emerged with his trousers soiled. A typical bully, he was an utter coward when it came to confrontation. He had pissed and shat himself with pure fear.

Liam looked at me. We were gobsmacked.

'Fucking hell, Jacko. They'll never dare fucking touch you again,' he said.

I was dazed. Nobody had ever stood up for me like this before. It was like a dream come true.

From that day on, I swore boxing saved my life. Those men were already my role models, but now I'd have died for them. To this day I thank them, because none of the carers dared lay a finger on me after that. Later, I heard the hospital had informed social services of my injuries, but when they investigated Bill Starling simply told them I'd fallen and hit my head. Nobody thought to question this.

*

Through boxing, it was the first time we started to have aspirations. The following week, on the way to our session, we talked as we ate our bread and chips.

'If we make it as pros, we could eat this every day, couldn't we?' I said to Liam.

'Nah, they eat steak, Jacko,' he laughed.

'When we go pro, Cathy and Alan can have front row seats,' I said. 'They can see us on the telly maybe?'

'They can watch us become champs,' Liam agreed. 'Shall we get a flat together too?'

I loved this idea. 'Yes!' I said. 'And go out and get lots of birds too.'

We both fell silent, lost in our future world. The fact we were even having these daydreams was amazing, as most kids in care never allow themselves that.

After our session, Cathy gave me a poster of Muhammad Ali, which I proudly put up on the wall next to my bed. Every night I'd go to sleep looking at him, imagining what he was like. By now he was a heavyweight champion of the world. When he was in a fight the country came to a standstill; the streets emptied and roads were deserted. Even the kids at St Leonard's fell silent for long enough to watch him fight. I was enthralled by everything about him. Not only his fighting, but also what sort of a man he was. He stuck up for himself and his beliefs, like speaking out against the Vietnam War and racism. Even at a young age I understood he could have easily ridden out the war – no way would they have put him on the front line. But instead he chose to stand up against it. I loved him for his quiet dignity, his ability to know right from wrong and the way he did what he believed in. Even as a kid I sensed he was a good man, a good adult.

He became almost like a father figure to me, a fantasy one, but someone I could look up to, alongside my boxing coaches.

Chapter 9: School's Out

Our nice little side-earner selling loot from Debenhams went well… until one day we got caught. Basically we'd got too cocky and set up our stall too close to where we'd nicked the stuff from, and a store detective spotted us.

'Oi, you two!' a voice yelled.

We looked around to see the dopey store detective. We'd stolen from under his nose many times before, but he'd finally twigged. We ran for our lives, dropping pens and lighters like a trail, not stopping until we reached The Chase. Then we lay down in the grass, laughing and catching our breath.

'That fat cunt wasn't ever gonna catch us, you know,' Liam laughed.

'Too right,' I agreed.

'We're too fast for him,' he grinned.

We lay on our backs for a moment, looking at the sky as a stream of birds flew past.

'Shame we can't do that no more. The stall is finished now,' I said.

'Finished?' said Liam. 'Nah, we can do it again! I ain't giving up on it, Jacko. No way!'

This was typical Liam. Fearless, determined Liam. He never wanted to stop, even when it was time to do so.

'Nah, we can't though, Liam. Now the store detective has clocked us he'll know who we are, won't he?'

He thought about this for a moment and then reluctantly nodded. Typical Liam – he never thought things through. It was up to me to work out the tactics, whatever we did.

More kids had cottoned on to Bill and Ted's kind offer for earning pocket money too, so we had to think of other ways of earning money. I got a paper round as soon as I was old enough, and we kids at the home also had jobs delivering leaflets in the local area. Turned out this was another scam. Not only were the staff creaming off the food budget for themselves, but they were getting us to work for free and then taking the money for extras.

Not having that extra cash was awful. We couldn't eat much again and the hunger began the next day. It made your tummy hurt and your head ache. I started to obsess about food, even dreaming of sitting down and eating proper meals like I had done at Mary's house or that afternoon I'd spent with my friend from school.

The only other person in my life who'd helped me was Mary, but it was around this time I decided to drop contact with her. It felt as if my life was taking me down a very different route to hers. By now she'd had another son, called Spencer, who was six years younger than me (so I was too old to play with him). I knew they were a nice family, living a nice life, and I felt like I no longer belonged anywhere near them. I was in survival mode all the time, and I'd felt like a stranger in their good family home during the last visit the previous summer. Although Mary hadn't changed, I had. Gone was the sweet little boy who loved riding Cloud, her horse. In his place was Jacko the fighter, the angry little boy growing into an angry young man. For a long time, Mary carried on writing me letters, asking me how I was. I just never replied to any of them. I felt Liam was the only family I needed, and my boxing coaches, who gave us support, advice and even clothes sometimes.

Now, we never quite understood how the ABC gym made any money because they never asked us for any. At first I thought they just felt sorry for us as we were from the care home, but actually I learned that few boys paid any fees. Lorries would come and go at all times, and sometimes designer goods would turn up. Alan used to hand us things like Ralph Lauren polo shirts, an incredible gift as we always wore the cheapest, dullest clothes you can imagine. I remember only having one set of clothing for the weekend.

'Go on, boys, have these,' he said, chucking us the shirts, still in their packaging.

'Fucking hell, it's proper designer,' said Liam, holding up a red polo shirt.

'Yeah, good bit of swagger that. Now off you go, son. Keep it,' Alan smiled.

I didn't lose any sleep over what the coaches were doing outside of the club, as they were so encouraging of me. Cathy always fed us up too, bringing in starchy food like cakes, pasties, sausage rolls, anything to give us the calories we craved.

But despite having the boxing club on my side, by the age of fourteen I was pretty much feral. Thanks to Alan threatening Starling, I no longer faced any beatings at the home, except from the other kids – and I constantly picked fights with them, especially the bigger ones, always people I'd decided 'deserved it'. Teachers at school still thrashed me whenever they liked too, so when I did turn up I always got the cane or worse.

Then one day, Mr Singh, who was still one of the biggest bullies I'd ever come across, crossed my path on a bad day. Like always, he was walking up and down the school corridor at break looking for the slightest excuse to wallop someone with his cane. As I walked past him, he budged into my shoulder.

'Connolly!' he yelled. 'Apologise immediately for barging into me.'

I spotted his hand twitching, preparing to start beating me. But this time I'd had enough.

'I ain't saying sorry, because you're the one who walked into me,' I snapped.

He grabbed my elbow to jostle me down the corridor.

'You insolent little prick,' he began, trying to make me walk at speed to a classroom. I knew what to expect: he'd use that cane with full brutal force away from everyone.

Now this guy was a good six foot two and built like a brick shit house, and kids had spent years petrified of him and his weapon. And I was sick of it. I twisted my arm to loosen his grip and then spun around, light on my feet like I was in the boxing ring, fists at the ready.

'Fuck off, you fat cunt!' I cried.

He raised his cane to strike me, but I was too fast for him. After ducking out of the way, I struck him square in the face, knocking him over like a bowling pin. For the split second before he fell, I noticed a look on his face I'd never seen before.

Surprise and fear.

Brilliant, I thought, almost smiling at him as he lay on the floor bleeding. *You fucking deserved that.*

Kids passing by stopped and stared, absolutely dumbstruck. But this was for them as much as it was for me.

Mr Singh pulled out a tissue to mop the dribble of blood running over his top lip.

'You'll pay for this, Connolly,' he snarled.

I didn't know what to do, so I walked on to my next class. I didn't need to wait long, though, as the head teacher came for me. Knowing I was for it, I followed him to his office.

'From today, you're expelled. Leave at once,' he said simply. 'I'll let St Leonard's know our decision.'

And that was that. At the age of fourteen, my education was finished. I held my head high as I walked out of the gates for the last time. Then I pulled off my polyester school tie, flicked my lighter and watched it go up in flames.

'Fuck that,' I said into the smoke.

Fuck the teachers, fuck the school, fuck the whole fucking system.

What a graduation. I was unable to read or write. All school had given me was more anger at the world.

I walked back to St Leonard's. I didn't need to worry about what Uncle Bill would say, because he was too afraid of the consequences of disciplining me. Of course, Auntie Coral gloated when she heard the news of my expulsion.

'Ah, Connolly, just one step away from being a jailbird now, ain't you? Too fucking stupid for school, yeah?' she spat.

*

The next step was for me to get a job. Many of the kids from the home left school without doing their O levels. They either returned to East London – to their dysfunctional families, if they had any – or found low-paid jobs and continued living at St Leonard's. Kids as old as twenty stayed at the home because, as well as being emotionally underdeveloped, many of us were clueless about the practical stuff. We had nobody teaching us the basic things someone in a normal home would see every day, like how to make a cup of tea, cook the most basic food or change a light bulb. Growing up in an institution keeps you away from so many things 'normal' people take for granted. Besides, I think Starling liked some of the bully kids staying so they could help control the younger ones. He'd often hand out cash or fags in exchange for the older ones beating up younger ones.

Luckily for me, I had my boxing coaches to step in. Alan and Lenny took me aside and told me their friend, Frank, needed help on his fruit and veg stall.

'It's just helping out selling stuff. You'll be alright at that, Jacko. He's a nice guy,' said Alan.

As far as I was concerned, if they said so, I could trust them one-hundred per cent, so I started working there the next day. At first I found it fun, bantering with shoppers and seeing how much I could sell. Frank seemed alright, a cockney geezer who was a hard man but good to me. Best of all, it didn't matter that I couldn't read, as I could tell an apple from a pear and deal with money, so nobody need know. However, it didn't take long to realise something else was going on. It wasn't just fruit and veg we were selling. There was obviously another business going on under the counter, one which the Old Bill would be very interested in. The packages involved were much smaller, but the wads of money were handed over in bundles.

About a week after I started, a nervous-looking guy approached the stall asking for Frank, who didn't seem best pleased to see him. He dragged the guy off to an alleyway and knocked seven bells out of him, and then the man scarpered. He returned the next day with money for Frank, who looked happy with himself.

Wow, I thought. *Nobody messes with these blokes.*

Just like Alan, Tommy and Lenny.

For the first time I thought how wonderful that would feel – to have that much respect from every man on the street. Little did I know that learning from men who demanded respect by using their fists would be the beginning of an addiction for me, one that I'd struggle with for half of my life. An addiction to violence.

*

By now it was blindingly obvious the boxing coaches were paying me more attention than Liam. During one session they spent ages with me in the ring, while my best mate was just throwing punches on the bag alone. Out of the corner of my eye, I saw him working himself up into one of his rages.

Bam. Bam. Bam. His fists sank into the bag.

I bet he's imaging that's my head, I thought. I didn't like my friend feeling left out, but there wasn't much I could do about it. Truth was, I was better at boxing techniques than him, and I couldn't stop them taking me more seriously than him, could I?

But I could see he was growing more impatient as I went into the ring for my session. In between punches I kept looking over at him.

Bam. Bam. Bam.

Then he turned to me and caught my eye.

'You want to fuck your mum, Cathy,' he mouthed clearly. 'Up. The. Bum.'

Liam knew what buttons to press and immediately I lost it and leapt out of the ring.

'Shut up. Just fucking shut up,' I snapped, fists flying.

But my mate soon had me on the floor and gave as good as he got. Fact was, he was still bigger and stronger than me, and in a brawl he'd always win. We laid into each other for a few seconds before others stepped in.

Cathy had overheard Liam's teasing and once the coaches had pulled us off each other she told Liam off.

'You need to fucking stop it,' she said. 'It's gone too far, Liam.'

Luckily Alan hadn't overheard what Liam said. If he had, he'd have gone mad.

For a whole week, Liam and I didn't speak. We ignored each other at breakfast and said nothing in training. Alan was the first to notice.

'Normally you two are like shadows. What the fuck are you two annoyed about? Fallen out over a girl?'

I didn't reply. I would never have grassed Liam up.

Then, the next session, we looked at each other and started laughing over nothing. There was no need for any apologies or any of that. We just needed to forget about it.

By now I was winning fight after fight, and was rapidly making a name for myself. The coaches took it so seriously they would pick us up from the children's home when we were taking part in competitions. Bill Starling would hide when they came, but neither he nor Auntie Coral missed the chance to put us down on the way.

'You're wasting these people's time with your shitty boxing games,' said Coral. 'Who do you think you are, Muhammad Fucking Ali, you cunt?'

I so badly wanted to punch her lights out and it always took every ounce of willpower not to do it. Instead, I'd jump into the car and we'd drive off. Knowing I had Alan watching my back meant the world to me.

One weekend, Liam asked me to go to the pub with him. He'd started to join other boys in their late teens, like Lawrence, drinking and trying to chat up girls. Lawrence, who always had an eye for the ladies, was now one of the biggest flirts of the group and had sussed out which local girls were easy and where they hung out.

'Come on, Paul,' Liam begged. 'Come pull some birds with me. There's some real nice ones out tonight.'

But it just didn't interest me. I got more from boxing than the thought of kissing girls in the pub. I didn't like drinking either: the taste of it was awful and, while others loved the feeling of being drunk, being out of control didn't appeal. In fact, being out of control made me feel worse rather than better.

Liam punched me on the shoulder. 'Come on, Jacko,' he ribbed.

But I shook my head. 'Nah, not today.' And I set off for training alone.

On the way I thought about how we were slowly drifting apart. Now I'd left school, we never walked to school together. And for someone who had been in care for so long, Liam was a really smart kid. He'd even learned to read a bit and made it to the mainstream. For the first time I wondered if our lives might go in different directions.

*

Now we were older, Liam and I often stuck up for the little kids. If we caught a member of staff being horrible, we'd step in and say something. I tried to reassure the little ones in my dorm as much as I could too. The worst thing was hearing them crying at night in their beds when they first arrived at St Leonard's. I mean, we'd all been through it, but somehow listening to another kid suffering was worse. It's that moment of realisation that nobody cares about you. You have nobody in the whole world who will protect you, who loves you just for you. It's a feeling every kid in care has had to deal with.

Much of the abuse had always been done behind closed doors, but finally, now I was older, the Snatch Squads stopped coming into my dormitory. I just wouldn't have allowed it to happen, and my reputation as a thug meant adults thought twice about coming in. Quickly, my cottage got a reputation as a safe place to be.

I also started to enjoy teaching the kids how to box, punching the air in front of them, and how to use their feet. Spending time on these mini lessons proved popular and we easily whiled away a boring Saturday afternoon when nobody had much to do.

Then, one day, I was involved in a fight outside the home that proved to me what I was capable of. I was with Michael, Lawrence and a few others waiting for a bus when we spotted some middle-aged blokes. Michael, the joker, had a mouth on him and he started on one of them.

''Ere, will you take a look at the hair gel on that old bloke? Who does he think he is? Elvis fucking Presley?'

We all laughed our heads off. It was true; one of the guys had a Teddy Boy look about him.

'Fuck off, you black cunt,' yelled one of the men.

Michael ran up to him. 'Fuck off yourself,' he shouted as he ducked and dived with his fists up. He never actually laid into the geezer, though, who turned to me.

92

'And why the fuck are you hanging around with all these black cunts?' he said.

'What?' I demanded, squaring up to him.

'You heard,' said another man. 'What's a white boy like you doing hanging around with a load of fucking black cunts?'

I felt rage grow inside of me straight away. These 'black cunts' were like brothers to me, number one. And, number two, I had never thought of or seen the world in a racist way, so I couldn't believe my ears. As an Irish boy in a kids' home, being white meant being in the minority and I genuinely didn't notice the colour of someone's skin.

'What the fuck?' I shrieked, approaching the man.

We were nose to nose, but he started jeering at me. 'Don't make sense!' the guy continued. 'A white boy around black kids.'

Without thinking, I raised my hand and slapped him as hard as I could. I never thought he'd fall, but he did, backwards, landing in a heap on the ground. Laughing, we all ran away. I laughed with the others, but my heart was racing. I'd never struck a stranger, a fully grown adult, like that before and the power felt incredible.

When I reached my dormitory, I saw one of the few nice members of staff, a man called Grant (I'll never forget him, as he had a hook for a hand).

'What's up, Paul?' he asked. 'You're quiet.'

'Ah, I just feel a bit bad for knocking over an old fella outside,' I replied.

'Why you do that?' he said.

I explained the situation and to my surprise Grant nodded and agreed with what I'd done.

'They shouldn't have said that to your friends,' he said. It was a very rare moment of support from a member of staff.

Around this time, I was very relieved to have been able to prevent another incident happening. Although Starling now left me to my own devices, I knew full well abuse would still be going on behind closed doors. Each set of house parents were laws unto themselves. The only time I saw inside other dorms was when I still waved at Liam from the window at night before bed. On this occasion, I was walking past Starling's staff quarters when I heard a noise, like a struggle. So I poked my head in.

'Fuck off, Paul,' Starling snapped when he saw me. Bill Starling was on top of Sonia, a thirteen-year-old girl with big blue eyes, who lots of the boys fancied. His fat, hairy hand was over her mouth as he tried to tug at her clothes. She twisted her head to look at me, her eyes wide with terror.

'What's going on?' I cried.

'Fuck off, I said,' snarled Bill. 'This is none of your business.'

'I ain't going anywhere,' I said. 'Get the fuck away from her.'

He continued pinning her down as he sat up to shout at me.

'This is none of your fucking business,' he began.

But there was no way I was walking away from such a blatant attack. So many of the rapes that went on were carried out behind closed doors. Rape was rarely seen in full view like this, but no way was I turning a blind eye to it. Fuck that.

Bill let go of her, leaping up to confront me. But my fists were at the ready. He tried to punch me, but I ducked and punched him on the cheek instead. We tussled for a bit and then he lost his balance.

Watching this beast go down was a pivotal moment. I mean, this was the man who had bullied me since the age of eight and who had made so many sad little kids' lives hell. I could have beaten the shit out of him there and then, but he looked like such a pathetic figure on the floor, scrabbling to his feet, that something stopped me.

Furious, he rose and he pulled at the heavy wooden wardrobe so it fell on top of me. I was knocked to the floor. But with a rush of adrenalin, I didn't feel a thing. I shunted it off me and stood up again, ready for round two. He looked at me weirdly, like he wasn't expecting me to get up.

'Do you want more? Do you?' I snapped at him furiously.

I saw genuine fear on his face and he backed away, before turning and half-running.

'Yeah, that's right, fuck off. Run away. Bye bye, you disgusting cunt.'

I watched him go; amazed I'd seen him off. I turned back to Sonia.

'He'd have raped me if you'd not come in,' she sobbed.

'You're safe now,' I said.

I never told Alan Mayhew about the beating as I had fended Starling off myself. It was unspoken, but we both knew he'd never lay a finger on me ever again, and he never did. This fight was a watershed moment for me. For a split second under that wardrobe I felt like I was invincible. Whatever happened physically, I didn't fear being hurt, I realised, and so now there was absolutely nothing to be scared of. This attitude was to stand me in good stead in the boxing ring, but in real life it became a disaster.

Many years later, when the home was investigated for abuse during Operation Mapperton, Sonia testified against Bill Starling during the trial at the Old Bailey. She said if I hadn't walked in and caught him that day, she'd have been raped.

Chapter 10: Growing Up

After eighteen months of working on the fruit and veg stall, I lost my job: Frank told me he couldn't afford to keep me on. But, luckily, the boxing coaches stepped in again.

'You can be a roofer,' Lenny said. 'We have a job for you in a proper company. It'll be more manual work, but you'll do well, boy.'

Once again I was so grateful to them. I could earn money now and carry on with the amateur boxing. I was sixteen, but life outside the home still felt like a great big unknown. Like most kids in care, I rarely thought about my future, but it went around that to qualify for a council flat you'd have to move back to the Tower Hamlets area. Liam told me that's what he planned to do, move back to East London and get a flat.

'What about our flat together?' I asked him.

'Yeah, we can still do that, Jacko,' he said. 'Just not around here.'

I wasn't sure if I liked that idea. Not being able to read meant I felt very cautious about going anywhere new, even if it was just ten miles up the road. I feared change. In fact, I feared pretty much everything still. When you can't read road signs or even pub names, your world becomes very small. The only areas I knew were Hornchurch, Romford and Dagenham, so that's where I planned to stay.

While Liam carried on at school for a bit, I enjoyed my new job and quickly learned the trade. Despite fearing the future, I was actually fearless up on the roof, jumping from scaffold to ladder, light-footed – partly because I didn't care if I lived or died.

By now, we were told to exist pretty much independently at the home. We had to buy our own food, learn to cook our own meals and do our own washing and ironing. As older kids, we were given cubicles for some privacy in the dorms too. But even if I could shut the door on my dormitory, I continued trying to reassure the little ones who arrived, wide-eyed and scared.

'Do the Snatch Squads come here?' they'd ask, peering around the cottage windows.

'You can go to bed and go to sleep in my dorm,' I'd assure them. The look of relief on their little faces was immense.

The best thing now was that the staff feared me, as they did lots of the older kids. Now, I can see how the staff created monsters in the children and then became afraid of them, leaving the most violent kids alone. Of course, they could have overpowered me in a group if they'd wanted to, but all the staff knew I'd fight to the death as I had nothing to lose. I'd have happily waited behind a door and slit their throats if they'd dared try to come in my dorm and take any kids sleeping there. In fact, I wouldn't even allow staff to just barge in without knocking. If any did, they'd get short shrift.

'Paul...?' one of the little ones would say if someone didn't knock, and I'd glance up from whatever I was doing and confront them.

'What the fuck are you doing here?' I'd ask, even if it was a domestic member of staff dropping off bed linen. 'Didn't anyone ever tell you to knock?'

I often tried to comfort young twins, Lenny and Tony. They cried at night for their parents because they weren't allowed home.

'Why are we still here?' they sobbed. 'We hate it.'

I didn't know the story of why their parents couldn't care for them, but they did get to have home visits and the plan was that one day they'd go home. I explained this gently to them.

'Come on, you've got to pull yourselves together, you two,' I'd say. 'You'll get out one day. You're not lifers like the long-stay kids.'

At other times, the bullying against younger kids was so malicious it quickly got nasty. One kid called James was playing with the card school and he won unexpectedly. As he walked off with a few quid, one of the older kids tried to steal his cash. I didn't hesitate to jump in, fists flying, to teach that fucker a lesson. Not only did bullies deserve it, but the truth was I got a buzz from doing it too. Whereas everyone else was smoking weed, sniffing glue, cutting themselves or having sex with anyone and everyone, I loved the thrill of a fight. I loved teaching fuckers who I thought deserved it a lesson. Seeing someone frightened of me boosted my self-esteem. But, instead of being bullied, I was rapidly becoming the bully.

While I got my own cubicle, some of the groomed kids got their own separate caravans on-site. There was very obvious favouritism still going on. Simon had one, and even moved his girlfriend into it – Leonie, a local girl who I assumed knew nothing about what was going on with Prescott. Simon continued to be the self-assured lad he was before. He always appeared to be someone in control of his life, even with Prescott sniffing around him.

Alongside having my own space, my need for control was coming out in a different way: OCD (obsessive-compulsive disorder). I still have it today. It's all about controlling elements of your environment when in your life you have very little control. Firstly, I started to neatly line up all my toiletries along the shelf next to my bed. If any were out of place, I panicked. I'd ball up one of my socks too and place it behind the door, so I could tell if anyone had dared step over the threshold. If they did, I'd go nuts. Then I filed my nails down to the skin, until they bled, and I became very meticulous about personal hygiene. I always planned my visits to the bathroom with care, though. After being beaten up for not cleaning the bath, I still had flashbacks and feared someone would be lying in wait to get at me. Even today I can't have a bath and relax in it. What a legacy.

As a kid without any background, I desperately wanted my own identity. So I found a tattoo parlour above an amusement arcade that didn't ask for ID and got a British Bulldog done, very fashionable in those days. All teenagers go through phases to find out who they are, but mine were desperate. I felt an unbearable need to fit in, so I embraced the skinhead movement, including all the punk-rock music and fashions, as if my life depended on it. I still didn't know much about my Irish heritage or who I was, but I could jump on this bandwagon like a 'normal' person and it felt wonderful.

Loads of other boys loved the mod scene too, and any money we could lay our hands on went on proper clothes, like Fred Perry shirts, and music. I always remember Lawrence being different, though, with his smart jumpers and trainers. He was what people called a 'casual' then, alongside all the mods, punks, skinheads and rockers. We all started to identify with something bigger than the identity of an unwanted kid from St Leonard's.

To date I have more than ten tattoos and to an outsider I might look like a racist, but in those days it was part of the scene to be patriotic. I also wanted to distance myself from my Irish heritage; after all, what had Ireland ever done for me aside from reject me? It would take many years before I reached out to those roots.

Considering how much of a misery St Leonard's made my life, it might make no sense that I stayed on beyond the age of sixteen. Legally we were old enough now to walk out and never return. But the problem was, most of us had nowhere to go and all of us were so clueless about the big, bad world that we felt frightened about trying to live independently. Add on the fact that our self-esteem was non-existent thanks to the extreme verbal abuse and I for one couldn't see a future. After all, Auntie Coral had been telling me for the best part of a decade by now that I didn't have one. We were, essentially, institutionalised. Our prisons today are filled with kids from care homes because they know nothing different.

One day, around this time, I was about to set off for training when I knocked on Liam's cottage door.

'You coming?' I asked him.

He'd missed the last couple of sessions and I didn't want him to fall even further behind. I was always being put up for fights and there was even talk of me going professional soon. Liam wasn't on my level anymore, but boxing was still our thing. But the look on his face told me he wasn't coming.

'Nah, Jacko, I ain't bothering with that shitty little boxing club anymore. Why would I? Not when there's beer and nice birds to be had,' he shrugged.

'What really?' I couldn't pretend to hide my disappointment.

'Yeah, Jacko, seriously. We've got some right dirty birds we're meeting later. Can't you miss training just for one fucking night? You always fucking win, so what's the point anyway?'

In all honesty, that felt a bit like a punch in the guts. Then Tommy's words echoed around my head.

'If you put everything into this, and I mean everything – not girls, not your social life, not the pub – then one day I think you've really got what it takes to make it big.'

'Nah, I have to go to boxing, Liam,' I said. 'See ya later.'

'What's the matter with you?' Liam said as I walked away. 'Are you fucking gay or something, Jacko?'

After that, I noticed nobody asked where my shadow was anymore. It was a given now that I'd come alone. Liam had dumped boxing, after about four years of us doing it together, and it hurt.

It was to be another year before I lost my virginity, aged seventeen, to a local girl who was a bit of a goer. A few boys had been with her, so I chatted her up one day and we had sex. Afterwards, the first person I told was Liam.

'Ah, Jesus Christ, thank fuck for that,' he laughed. 'I thought you were going to die a fucking virgin.'

We both laughed and it felt like old times, briefly. That day we hung out until Liam went off to the pub and I went off to training. By now, Liam had also befriended a local family and he often disappeared to get fed and experience some normal family time. I was pleased for him, even if I craved it myself and it meant we were growing further apart.

Happily for me, though, my own taste of being part of an ordinary family was about to happen. At this time I was working part-time at a menswear shop in Romford that sold clothes to thugs, skinheads and mods. It was run by two Jewish geezers who paid a pittance, but I didn't care as I loved the fashion. Not being able to read or write didn't matter either, as my sales banter made up for it. One afternoon, I was walking to work when I spotted a couple of skinhead girls hanging about. One of them, a pretty blonde called Lindsey, shouted at me.

'You've got the two best things I like in a boy,' she said. 'Nice eyes and a nice arse.'

I looked at her as she dissolved into giggles.

'How old are you?' I asked, finding her confidence attractive.

'Sixteen,' she said.

She was a normal girl from a normal family, so I was flattered she had time for the likes of me. I asked her out and was thrilled when she said yes.

I didn't have much money, so we couldn't afford meals out or trips to the cinema, so she brought me home to meet her parents, Val and Dave at their house opposite the boxing club. Suddenly I was very tempted myself to miss training, as all I wanted to do was be with her.

Socially I still struggled, but luckily I found her parents really easy to talk to and they seemed to find me charming. Her dad was a copper at Barkingside Police, but even he gave me, a kid from the home who'd never amount to anything, the time of day.

Lindsey and I became inseparable, and I spent all my free time, when I wasn't at work or in the gym, at her house. We were soon having sex, even with her parents in the house. They made me lovely hot meals and I felt taken care of for once.

One evening I got talking to Val about leaving school early. She made me feel so at ease, I even admitted I couldn't read or write.

'Oh, Paul. You're clearly such a bright boy. That school really let you down, didn't it?' she said.

I shrugged. I never dwelt on things like that. I just wanted to put it all behind me.

'Hmm,' she said. 'How would you feel if I helped try to teach you how to read?' she offered. 'We could start with the basics and go from there?'

And so some evenings after dinner, when I wasn't upstairs shagging Lindsey, I'd be sitting at the dining-room table trying to learn to read with her mum. I found it very hard work and must have tested Val's patience. I soon gave up, as it proved impossible, but she managed to teach me a few words.

Even if I was definitely a lad from the wrong side of the tracks, the Whyte family showed me how a nice, 'normal' family worked. I never really felt like I belonged, but it was wonderful to be part of the family.

About a year later, I bought Lindsey a fake diamond ring and asked her to marry me. She said yes straight away and we vowed to be together forever. But, sadly, it wasn't long before my background caught up with me.

It all began one night, just after the little kids were put to bed in my dormitory. One of the black kids came home from a visit to East London and brought a load of his rough mates with him. They were hanging about with one of those huge ghetto blasters, waking up the little kids. Of course, all the staff, including Bill Starling, were nowhere to be seen. Being classic bullies, they could only take on people smaller and weaker, not a bunch of teen thugs. So it was up to me to take action.

'What the hell is going on? Fuck off away from our cottage,' I said to the lads. 'And turn that shit down.'

'Says who?' asked one of them. 'Fuck off yourself.'

'I don't think so,' I yelled. Unable to resist the urge to attack, I went straight for him.

Smash!

It was one strong blow and he fell backwards, landing in a satisfying heap.

Job done, I thought and turned to walk away. I wanted to get back to the little kids to reassure them they could sleep.

But just then I felt a warmth spreading over my stomach. I turned around and saw a kid standing with a Stanley knife he'd just used to stab me. I held on to the wound to stem the flow of blood as all the kids ran off. Someone called an ambulance and I was rushed off on a stretcher.

'You okay, Paul?' voices said as I started to feel sick. I had no idea if I was badly hurt, but I didn't regret stepping in. My role as a big brother figure and protector was important.

At the hospital, as I waited to be stitched up, the police insisted on speaking to me before the doctors treated me.

'We need to know who did this,' one asked. 'So we've come to take a statement.'

Now, after so many years, I didn't trust anyone in authority, least of all a copper, even if Dave had taught me that not all of them were bad. I didn't see myself as a snitch either, so I shook my head.

'I ain't making any statement,' I said. 'Okay?'

'No, that isn't okay,' replied the copper. 'No statement. No treatment.'

So I lay there, my blood soaking the piece of gauze given to me on arrival at A&E, waiting for treatment that the police were preventing me from having! Nothing surprised me by now, however. I had spent my whole life being let down by the authorities, from social workers to teachers to care home staff. After a while I started to feel woozy and sick. I just wanted to get back to my bed. Then I heard a familiar voice.

'What's happening here? Get this boy seen to immediately. You can't deny him treatment, for God's sake!'

It was Lindsey's dad, Dave. He'd heard of a stabbing at St Leonard's and come to check out who it was. He ranted about how I was the victim here and how wrong it was of the police to try to force me to give a statement.

Quickly, doctors stitched me up and Dave took me back to his house to let me sleep on their sofa. I was so grateful to him for stepping in, but he wouldn't hear a word of it.

'It's a disgrace to the force the way they behaved around you,' he said.

Lindsey was horrified to see me injured. She and Val couldn't have been kinder and they made a fuss of me.

The next day they dropped me back at St Leonard's, where I was staying in Simon's caravan for a few days, as he was away with Leonie. As Lindsey said goodbye, I'd never been more grateful for our relationship. Watching her dad drive off, I thought how it must look, me stabbed in the stomach and living in a caravan in some kids' home field. But at last I'd met someone who could overlook my rough beginnings.

Sadly, my relief wasn't to last. The next day, her dad's car turned up and Lindsey jumped out.

'I'm really sorry, Paul. I don't think things are gonna work out,' she said.

I didn't say much. After all, what could I say? What dad would want his daughter to be knocking around with a lad like me?

'Sorry,' she mouthed as I watched her be driven off again. Devastated, I secretly hoped she'd change her mind.

Then the next day a letter arrived. Auntie Coral picked it up before I had a chance to open it.

'Aww, what's this, Paul?' she said gleefully. 'Let me see. A little break-up note? Poor fucking thing. You can't even read it, can you? So shall I? "Dear Paul, I am really sorry things haven't worked out. I really loved you, but it's just not right anymore…" Aww, you fucking Irish cunt, why am I not surprised? Nobody loves you, Paul. Nobody ever has.'

And so she went on and on, until other kids started laughing. Then, when she saw I was upset, she threw the letter at me. I grabbed the paper, cussing her, and went to lie on my bed. Of course, Auntie Coral was right, I couldn't read it, and this made me feel even worse.

*

For weeks I was heartbroken and didn't know what to do with myself. Lindsey had been the first girl I loved, and more than that, I'd liked her family too. They were decent people who'd helped me. Dave had even suggested I sign up with the police cadets like he had. For the first time I'd felt like I was worth something, and now, bam, I was worth nothing again.

The only positive side to our break-up was my restored enthusiasm for boxing. I'd never stopped going but I'd started to sack off training to spend time with Lindsey. Now, with no distractions, I threw myself back into it.

By now, kids were leaving the home, including friends like Lawrence, who disappeared off to Stepney Green, back to where he originated from. Liam didn't stop talking about getting his 'flat' either. Although we'd drifted, I still loved him and we sometimes went for a few drinks together.

'You know, you'll get free carpets, white goods, start-up money and everything if you get a flat in East London,' he said. 'You won't get jack shit if you stay around here.'

He made East London sound like some sort of paradise. After being so badly looked after by the council for so long, we felt we were owed something. We'd all been abused for so long, the least the authorities could do was help set us up in the real world.

'Yeah, but I ain't going anywhere, Liam,' I said.

I'd made friends through work and was treated like one of the lads in the building community. For the first time, I'd started to feel like I might belong somewhere, especially working with people that Alan, Lenny and Tommy knew.

It wasn't always easy. I used to hide what I saw as my Achilles' heel, not being able to read. I'd sit in the cafes with them at lunchtime with a copy of *The Sun* like they did, staring at Sam Fox's boobs and pretending I knew what the headline said when people chatted about it.

'Nah, I've decided I'm staying here,' I said. My security was here, in this area. This was all I knew. I couldn't face starting again from scratch, even with Liam by my side.

He shrugged. 'Ah, you're a fucking mug, Jacko.' He grinned, punching my shoulder. I punched his back harder and we both burst out laughing.

Not long after, Liam left. I don't remember the last time we saw each other or spoke. Certainly, there was no proper goodbye. I would have just assumed we'd keep in touch, like he would have done, I expect. Sure, we'd drifted, but we were like brothers, had been through so much. I just heard from someone that a batch of kids had left, gone to East London to try to find their place in the world, and he was one of them.

Good luck to you, Liam, I thought when I walked past the frosted window of his cottage. *I'm pretty sure you'll fly whatever you do.*

Chapter 11: The Great Escape

My fear of leaving St Leonard's was very real. I didn't have a clue about where I'd go or what I'd do. The sad fact was, I didn't know my family and I felt I couldn't contact Mary after years of ignoring her letters. Having nobody and not being able to read meant trying to find a flat to rent was unthinkable. Somehow I managed to do a good job of faking confidence, but that's as far as my self-esteem went. Even today I have no solid sense of self-esteem. And if you don't have it aged fifty-five, you're not ever going to get it, are you?

By the age of nineteen, I was working part-time in Terminal Four, Heathrow airport, doing a roof on a building. There were lots of Irish workers there and on our lunch break we'd sit in the big canteen. One afternoon, this big ginger guy kept staring over at me.

'Think he fucking fancies you,' said one of the others.

'Fuck off,' I laughed, drinking my tea.

'Yeah, I think he fucking does too,' said another.

I looked up, ready for trouble, to see what they were on about. I had nothing against gay blokes, but I didn't want my mates ribbing me.

'What the fuck?' I said.

I couldn't lose face with anything, so I got up and marched over to this guy, who looked to be in his forties. He had a soft face and I wondered why he wanted to start something.

'What the fucking hell do you want?' I snapped.

'You're the chosen one,' he said quietly. 'You're a seventh son of the seventh son, aren't you?'

I sat down next to him and forced myself to laugh, but I couldn't stop staring at him now.

'What the fuck?' I began.

He nodded, gaining confidence as he knew he'd guessed correctly.

'The problem is you have too much aggression in you,' he tutted. 'Too much violence and spite. You'll lose that one day, though, and become a great healer later on in life.'

By now I was laughing in his face.

'Shut up! Me? A great healer?' I grinned. 'I can hardly get myself dressed in the morning, mate.'

The guy introduced himself as Tom and we started an unlikely friendship, often sharing a pot of tea at lunchtime. I took what he'd said with a pinch of salt, even if it had shocked me. How had he guessed? And what did this seventh son stuff mean? He told me it was a strong feeling he had and I should believe what he said to be true.

'Well, if I do have this lucky streak, I need it to start working now,' I laughed.

I suppose, looking back, this incident made me wonder about my past. All I'd heard from my siblings was how they'd struggled with their lives since leaving care. John had been locked up for mugging old ladies. Mick had gone off to live in a commune, got confused about his sexuality and turned to booze. Declan was working in some factory. Matty had done okay with a good job, but I never heard from him. Anne was the only one who stayed in touch with the odd phone call.

I didn't like staying in touch, as my family didn't make me feel good. I needed to carve my own path, away from all my tainted siblings. But, weirdly, to have a stranger say out of the blue that my place as the seventh son was lucky gave me hope. Perhaps my life might turn out okay in the end?

By now, it was 1981 and I'd been living in the home for eleven long years. We were institutionalised. Our 'house parents' still loomed as our biggest influencers, even if they were afraid of us. Then out of nowhere, one of them, Haydn Davies, disappeared.

'Haydn's got done for fucking Terence up the bum,' said Mark.

The news tore through the cottages like wildfire. Davies had been arrested for buggery and was on remand. Terence was a mixed-race rent boy from the West End, who'd arrived at St Leonard's 'for his own protection' years earlier. Like all the abused kids, he was a quiet one, withdrawn, and like Haydn's little lapdog, poor thing. I have no idea of Terence's background, but let's just say that for most rent boys being 'saved' from the streets and ending up at St Leonard's was like discovering the light at the end of the tunnel is an oncoming train.

I don't know the details of this case, as the files have never been released, but I even heard the police had filmed evidence. Terence disappeared too, presumably to another children's home. Nobody explained anything, of course, or got to say goodbye.

To start with kids were genuinely excited. Perhaps, after all, the police *did* care? Maybe someone else, like Starling, might get nicked next? Could this be the whole thing unravelling? But sure enough, any hope of justice soon disappeared. Starling continued ruling with an iron rod and Haydn's arrest was dismissed as a freaky, one-off incident.

We all assumed Haydn would never be seen again, so I was stunned to spot him hanging around the driveway about a year later. I don't know what job he had, but he was clearly working with us kids again – not in the same role, but he was still on-site for years to come.

*

When I turned twenty, I was working as a roofer and still living at St Leonard's. I was embarrassed and ashamed, but felt paralysed to do anything about it. Although I worked hard during the day and among colleagues I was quite popular, my whole Jack the Lad attitude was just a mask. Behind my smile and hard-working ethic, I felt like the piece of shit I'd always been told I was. I just didn't believe I could cope in the real world. I knew nothing about the basic ways to live a life, like how to drive, or pay bills, or find a place to rent. Not being able to read made it even more overwhelming. As much as I would have loved my independence and my own place to live, it felt impossible. I was stuck living in a kids' home I hated, but it was the only thing in my world I knew.

Then one day, any decision about leaving was made for me. And after hearing her whiny, critical voice for the past twelve years, it seems fitting it was Auntie Coral who made me snap. It started when she began ranting at me while I was trying to make spag bol, the only dish I know how to make to this day, in the kitchen.

'Can you fucking clean up after yourself, you lazy sod?' she began. 'Don't know how you think you can get away with living here like this. You're a fucking pig.'

I felt a red-hot anger stir deep within my guts. Now, there were many things to be said of me, but calling me lazy and untidy wasn't fair. I was struggling with raging OCD and I was a stickler for any untidiness to the point of absolute obsession. The few clothes I did have I made sure were immaculate and folded with military precision. I was obsessed by personal hygiene, always making sure I was as clean as possible, and I hated anything in my tiny cubicle being even a millimetre out of place. After so many years of abuse from this foul-mouthed bitch, something inside of me had had enough.

'Oh, just fuck off,' I yelled at her. 'Shut your fucking disgusting mouth.'

Although I'd often talked back to Coral before, I'd never screamed at her with such venom.

'Shut my mouth? You cunt, Paul. When are you leaving here, eh? You need to fuck off out of here and join the council waiting list like the rest of them. Prison fodder is all you are and is where you'll end up. Or dead! You were a shitty little kid and you've turned into a shitty little man,' she retorted. 'With a big chip on his shoulder.'

That was it. Without thinking, I lifted up the heavy wooden table I was making my food on and tipped it over. My split second fantasy was to squash her beneath it as if she was the Wicked Witch in *The Wizard of Oz*. I didn't know how far I'd go, but at the least I wanted to harm her so she could never, ever use that vile mouth of hers again.

She staggered backwards, the table landing by her feet and, to my disappointment, missing her completely. The look on her face was one of shock.

But that wasn't enough. I ran towards her like a bull seeing red.

'You fucking evil slag. I should rip your fucking head off, you bitch,' I screamed in her face.

My fists twitched with desperation to punch that horrible mouth of hers as hard as possible, but something inside stopped me.

Perhaps it was because she was a woman and I'd never hit someone weaker than me before. Perhaps it was because I feared if I began beating her, I might not ever stop. But her look of fright made me pleased. I'd given her a right scare.

'Go fuck yourself instead,' I screamed, before watching her run away.

Minutes later, one of the managers who did fuck all usually, appeared.

'My office now, please, Paul,' he said.

I followed him, still fuming about Coral. I knew I was going to get a dressing-down and the unfairness of it all was already gnawing away.

'Paul, you have to leave St Leonard's,' he said.

'When?' I asked.

'Today.'

'But I ain't got anywhere to go?' Instantly, I felt like a lost little boy again.

He shook his head. 'Well, this has gone too far. I've called the police. You can't stay here.'

My bravado evaporated and I was terrified. What did he mean? Where would I go?

'Well, you're twenty and an adult now,' said Jeff simply.

I waited until the police arrived and they had a brief chat with me. I told them how abusive Auntie Coral was, but predictably they weren't interested. Nobody was actually injured, so they didn't take any action. They just told me to be on my way, as Jeff had advised.

I told Jeff again I had nowhere to go, but he shrugged his shoulders. I could see he didn't care, but he said if I really needed it, I could spend one more night at St Leonard's. I got up and left, my mind racing.

Where should I start? The reality of being illiterate was terrible. I couldn't even read the small ads to find a flat or work out how to pay a deposit. I couldn't read my wage slips, maps, or instructions for anything. I couldn't visit areas outside of my routine in case I got lost. Once, recently, I'd even got confused over which pub to meet the lads in after work as I couldn't read the pub sign outside. I felt vulnerable and alone, so once again I went to the only people in the world who would be willing to help.

Dagenham Boxing Club.

I let my trusted coaches know what was happening and sure enough, the next day, a bedsit had been found and its rent paid for a month. Then my mate Trevor, the window dresser from the menswear shop, offered to pick me up and drive me there.

That last night I kept myself to myself. A few of the others my age were still there, poor kids like Leeroy, who after surviving such abuse was a shell of a person, and Mark Byrnes, who was still very emotionally immature. I was so scared but I didn't want to show it, so I just packed up my cubicle and tried to think positively. The day had come for me to go and there was nothing more I could do about it.

The next morning I woke up, had a meagre bowl of cereal and packed my bag. It didn't take long, as I still didn't have many belongings. Then I took down my beloved Muhammad Ali poster and I was ready. I walked out of my cottage without saying goodbye to anyone, with exactly the same small suitcase I had arrived with as an eight-year-old. It wasn't just emotional immaturity that stopped me saying goodbye to my dormitory, it was terror of what would happen next. All I'd ever heard of kids leaving St Leonard's was what a fuck-up their lives had been. Kids either ended up in prison, on the streets or in the army. Thinking for yourself and having to cope alone were unimaginable. All I could cling to now were my friends and my boxing life.

As I waited on the driveway, I was so grateful to see Trevor's car pull up. He wound down the window when he saw me.

'Come on, you wanker, get in. Let's get out of here,' he grinned.

We took off at speed, doing a handbrake turn on the driveway, and for a few seconds I felt excited. I was leaving St Leonard's behind forever! Maybe life on the outside wouldn't be so bad after all?

This feeling didn't last for long. As soon as we pulled up at my new pad, my heart sank. It was a shit house in a shit area. Not that I expected to be living in Buckingham Palace, I just thought it might be somewhere I could feel safe.

'It's only temporary, Paul,' said Trevor, punching me on the arm as if he'd guessed my thoughts. 'Just a stop gap until you find somewhere better.'

I thanked him and got out. 'See ya later, Trev. Thanks again for the lift,' I said, putting on a brave face.

As he sped off, I wanted to run after him, but I knew it was time to do this. Stand on my own two feet.

Minutes later, I'd met the homeowners and been shown to my tiny box room, with its filthy mattress and horrible wallpaper. The house rules included not being allowed to use the kitchen or the bathroom, so I had to use the tiny sink on one wall and eat out all the time. Trying to make the best of it, I unfurled my Muhammad Ali poster and stuck it on the wall by my bed. Then I sat on the grimy duvet and thought: *What now?*

A horrible feeling of loneliness crept over me as I listened to the silence of my new room called home. All of a sudden, I longed for the company of my dorm or to go into the dayroom and watch the TV. Just anything familiar.

I took a deep breath. I couldn't dwell on this, so I grabbed my coat, went out and got myself some dinner. That night it was from the fish and chip shop, the same one Liam and I went to at times. At least I had the security of knowing the area. Not for the first time I was pleased I'd made the decision not to follow all the other kids to Tower Hamlets and East London. I wouldn't have coped with living in a big city and leaving behind all the places I knew on top of everything else.

That night, with nothing better to do, I went to bed early. As I lay down I tried to relax, but I couldn't switch off. The security of my small room worried me. The door didn't have a lock on it. So I got up and wedged a chair underneath the handle and laid deodorant cans on top, so if anyone knocked it over I'd hear them. Then I lay back down, thinking of what tools I could take from work to help arm me tomorrow. A monkey wrench? A crowbar? Yes, I would make sure I was kitted out, just in case.

Don't ask me 'In case of what?' because I didn't know. The people who owned the house seemed fine and nobody knew I was here. But this was the point. I didn't need anything specifically to feel moments of terror. Being overcome with a feeling of dread was part of my psyche now. All of a sudden, for no reason, the sensation would envelop me. I'd feel my heart racing, my mouth go dry, as if I was about to die at any moment, and then, after a few minutes, it would pass.

Looking back today, I know these were symptoms of Post-Traumatic Stress disorder from years and years of growing up with the threat of violence hanging in the air everywhere. It's not something I could just snap out of, because my brain had developed when I was a young kid to expect something bad to happen and be ready to defend myself. Back then, as a young adult, I couldn't just switch this part of my brain off. I was suffering from flashbacks and sudden rushes of adrenalin for no reason at all. But night-times were even worse. Relaxing and nodding off knowing everything was safe in the world wasn't a feeling I was familiar with. I needed a weapon for that. So that first evening, after triple-checking the door, I nodded off with one eye half open.

I woke up after a bad night's sleep and tried to tell myself everything would be okay as I would get tooled up for the following night. I went to work as normal and put a brave face on it. I didn't want the lads to know that, inside, Jacko was insecure, so I laughed and joked as usual.

By the end of that day I'd made a big decision. Living outside of St Leonard's was going to be tough and I needed all my strength to do it. That meant staying away from my past. I didn't want to keep in touch with anyone, none of my brothers or my old dormitory friends. None of them were happy people and I wanted to escape it all. I needed to surround myself with good people not tainted by the horrors we went through. That included everyone, even Liam.

Chapter 12: Facing Facts

The one thing that helped me get through this period was what had saved my life years earlier. Boxing. Luckily I still had my training and I went as often as I could, taking it more seriously than ever. Once in a while I also got invited back to some of the other lads' homes, where their parents gave me a home-cooked meal. By now I was an Amateur Boxing Association champion, having won seventy-six out of eighty-four fights, so Tommy talked more about me turning professional.

'The games are very different, Jacko,' he explained. 'Pro boxing is twelve rounds compared to the amateur's three rounds, but you should go for it. I see a champion in you, boy.'

I knew he wasn't the sort to just say this. He'd spent years building me up and he believed in me, even when I didn't, or couldn't, believe in myself. I should have been proud. These achievements should have raised my self-esteem to what it needed to be. Don't get me wrong, Alan, Tommy and Lenny all praised me to the hilt, but after feeling good for about five seconds, the moment passed. I'd go home, look in the mirror and still feel like a piece of shit. I might have left the home and Auntie Coral behind, but somehow the bitch stayed somewhere in my head, telling me how unloved and unwanted I was in every situation I found myself.

At times I still struggled with the discipline of boxing too. It wasn't about being committed to the sport; I just couldn't seem to leave my temper outside the ring. I still got called out for it, even if I kept winning, either for headbutting or ducking too low. Most of it was accidental, but occasionally it wasn't.

Tommy pulled me aside one evening.

'I told you before,' he said. 'If you want to go pro, you have to clean up. You'll waste your whole career if you get known as a thug and you won't ever make the England squad. So c'mon, Jacko. Sort it.'

I knew he was right. If you got disqualified more than half a dozen times, you were blackballed and were only good for unlicensed fighting, something I definitely didn't want to get involved in. I listened to him and vowed to keep my temper in check, even if I had no clue how I would do this.

That night, as I lay on my bed with Tommy's words echoing in my head, I thought of me and Liam lying in the fields stuffing our mouths with chips, riding our horses and dreaming of one day going pro. I wished I could tell him I was one step closer.

*

A few days after leaving, I got a call from St Leonard's to say I needed to return to pick up stuff I'd left. Reluctantly I made a quick visit, not hanging around to speak to anyone. As I was leaving, Ron Wickham, the staff member who went on to marry the seventeen-year-old, pulled up in his old Ford Cortina.

'Hey, I'm flogging this old banger. Know anyone who might be interested?' he asked.

I shook my head but then suddenly had an idea.

'I'll have it!' I said. 'I'd love a car.'

Never mind I'd never driven one before, let alone had a licence or insurance. Impulsively, I just thought it was a good idea. I had some cash from payday, so I peeled off my wages from my back pocket. Ron shrugged, took the money and chucked me the keys.

'Good luck,' he said, counting the notes.

Crazy as it sounds, I just got in, worked out how to turn the key in the ignition and did a couple of laps of the field. Then, I bunny-hopped down the long drive of St Leonard's for the final time.

'Wahey!' I cried, turning the window down. I had a set of wheels! Reading road signs was tricky but thankfully I knew the area, so I just drove back to my bedsit and parked up.

Easy, I thought.

With my new set of wheels I felt more like a 'real man' and this felt important to fit into my new social circle. I'd met lots of lads from Dagenham in the building trade over the years and now they were the only people I hung out with. They accepted me for who I was, which was a pretty fucked up young adult. Because of the panic attacks, I could be sitting laughing and joking in the pub one minute and then suddenly overcome with a feeling something terrible was going to happen the next. This panic paralysed me out of the blue and I'd have to breathe it out in silence. But suddenly going quiet and staring at one spot intensely wasn't the sort of thing that went down well in a pub when you're bantering with mates or trying to chat up some bird. Some lads called me a weirdo and ribbed me for it.

'Oi, Jacko, cat got your tongue?'

'What's up with him? He looks like he's seen a ghost!'

Others, who I was closer to, like one of the guys called Psycho Sam, were a bit more understanding.

'What's up with you, Paul?' he asked me one time when I suddenly stopped talking mid-sentence.

He waited for a few seconds as I breathed, struggling to contain a terrible cold sweat.

'Ah, sorry, Sam,' I said finally. 'I was abused in my kids' home, beat up and that. Just something that happens now and then, innit.'

The look on his face told me he had no idea what 'abuse' meant. These mates of mine were from rough homes, but hadn't been neglected or beaten or witnessed sexual abuse. Back then this wasn't something you saw on telly, and nobody spoke about it either. I didn't go into detail, but I don't keep secrets either. I understood my panics were linked to being a kid, I just didn't understand why they happened. Counselling, let alone therapy, was just not something I thought about.

After I explained it to him, Psycho Sam often told the others to shut up when I had a freak-out.

'Jacko'll be alright, just buy him another beer or something,' he'd say.

And then the moment would pass and Jack the Lad would be back in the room, joking with the best of them.

Aside from these moments, from the outside I looked like the life and soul. But once the door was shut on my bedsit, my loneliness consumed me. Despite having lots of flings since Lindsay, I never met anyone I fell for and I was never able to commit. Sex was good, but love? Forget it. I just wasn't interested.

I was plagued by nightmares too, such as a recurrent one where I was trapped in a building and unable to find a way out. I even dreamt of beating up my biological mother, punching her square in the face over and over again until she became a bloody mess. I don't think I needed a dream analyst to work out what these things meant. Night-times were always the worst, lying alone in that horrible bedroom. After checking the door and window lots of times and making sure I had my trusty duster under my pillow, I physically ached with loneliness.

Sundays were my worst days, as the cafes were shut and nowhere did takeaways. So, feeling desperate, I found an old phone number for my sister, Anne. She lived in Basildon now and had married and had a son of her own. The first day I went around for Sunday lunch felt quite awkward. We made polite chit-chat but really she felt like a stranger still, even if I was grateful for the meal and company. She never asked me about life at St Leonard's and I never told her. I got the impression she struggled herself, as she constantly chain-smoked and looked on edge. Equally she never spoke about our birth mum or dad, even though she had more of a relationship with her than I ever did. I can only say I wasn't interested. That woman had never done anything for me and I knew she didn't care either. A few years later, Anne moved away with her family up north to Wakefield to set up a new business. She said goodbye and promised to keep in touch, but I rarely heard from her again.

Dealing with being illiterate felt so lonely too. Not being able to read in the 'real world' was a huge disadvantage and one I wasn't handling well. It wasn't just the little things like bills and newspapers I couldn't read. Big things got in the way too. Like when I tried to register with my local doctor, only to be faced with a form I couldn't read. In desperation, I admitted this to the receptionist. Now doctors' receptionists are not known for their friendly manner, but this one looked as if I'd called her mum a slag or something.

'Just fill out what you can then,' she snapped.

'But I can't,' I began.

She glared at me. 'Just do your best then.'

'But I can't read any of it,' I said quietly.

'Well, we don't have time to fill forms out for people who can't read,' she tutted as if I was the biggest inconvenience she'd come across all day. So I had to just sit and wait until someone was available.

Like everything, I kept my troubles secret. After all, who could I tell?

*

The only other person from my past I didn't quite leave behind was Simon, because he lived locally and every now and again I'd bump into him. I wasn't thrilled to see him, as I'd heard he was into heroin now, but out of all the poor kids from St Leonard's he was still the most switched on. Despite whatever had gone on with him and Prescott, he had the same swagger and confidence he'd always had. One day I saw him in town and we had our first proper chat.

'How's it going, Jacko?' he asked. 'Where you working now?'

I shrugged and told him about working back at the roofing company and my new pad. I didn't talk it up, but I didn't want him to think I was living in some shit hole either, even if that was the case. Like always, Simon was immaculately kitted out, wearing the latest trainers and jeans.

'How's it going?' I asked.

'Great! Me and Leonie married and we're expecting a baby,' he said. 'And I'm living on Victoria Road now.'

I knew the houses on Victoria Road were big, family council houses with gardens. Straight away I wondered how he'd managed to wangle one.

'Fucking hell,' I said. 'Nice road to live on!'

We all knew we were under a different council here to the care home and didn't stand a chance with the long waiting lists. He shrugged and mumbled something about Leonie's family helping him out.

One evening he invited me over to visit. I was amazed at what a proper nice place he had, with lovely furniture and carpets. Leonie got chatting to me too as she made a spag bol.

'We had Alan Prescott over the other night,' she said, stirring the mince. 'He had dinner with us.'

I felt my stomach tighten. Simon was always his favourite in the home, and I bet Prescott had pulled a few strings to land him this place. Prescott was a powerful man within the local authority. I wanted to say something to Leonie, but she seemed oblivious to it all and even liked Prescott as a person.

I also came to realise that although from the outside Simon's life looked good, from the inside it was a different story. He was now harbouring a very serious heroin addiction.

A few months later, I bumped into him again and he asked me for a lift to a flat in Dagenham. I felt I couldn't say no, so I took him to the address and he leapt out of the car.

'Thanks, mate,' he said. I looked up at the grim-looking flat where he was going and guessed he was picking up his next fix.

I glanced at him, wanting to say something. To talk to him about the drugs or how dangerous they were. But the problem was, Simon was one of the most self-assured people I knew and he was not going to listen to me, even if I did have his best interests at heart.

I decided not to hang around Simon after that. I just had to get away from people going down the wrong tracks if I was to stand any chance of a normal life at all.

Chapter 13: Two Faces

Meanwhile, I was too concerned with my own life to worry much about anyone else's. By now I'd had a few run-ins with coppers for driving a car with no insurance or licence. Unbelievably, one time I even managed to talk my way out of it when two coppers pulled me over.

'Right,' said one. 'Out of the car. You're coming with us.'

I laughed. 'If you two muppets think you can take me in, you need to think again. I'll tell you what, get on that radio and call for your mates to come and help, because you'll need help if you want to bring me in.'

Talk about asking for trouble, but my pride meant I wasn't going to turn myself in quietly. Then, to my shock, they took one look at me and decided I wasn't worth it.

'Okay, just get the relevant documentation for next time,' one said, and I left them standing in exhaust fumes looking like Pinky and Perky.

Of course, I took no notice whatsoever, as I had no extra money to pay for things like driving lessons, and I ignored the fact I'd been given a second chance. The next time I got nicked I'd left a petrol station at speed, only to skid straight into railings, which narrowly missed my head through the window. Back then, I'd never wear a seat belt either, thinking if I needed to jump out or someone came at me I'd be 'ready'. I always needed to be 'ready'. After this incident, a serious-looking letter landed on my doormat. I had to ask my mates to read it for me and they told me it was a summons to appear at Romford Magistrates' Court. Suddenly, Auntie Coral's prophecy swirled around my head again.

'You're just a Connolly, fucking prison fodder you! ... You'll end up dead or in prison, you little cunt.'

Maybe she was right? Maybe this time I'd had it? Of course, not having insurance doesn't usually warrant a prison sentence, but even a fine wasn't something I could afford.

On the day of the hearing, I didn't own a suit so I turned up in my smartest jeans and T-shirt. When I walked in, I held my head high, telling myself it was no big deal. I put on my best Jacko swagger, thinking this would all be over in an hour or so.

As I sat down, waiting for the magistrates to appear, I looked around the room. The Royal Courts of Justice were where so many of us kids end up, so I guessed this almost felt like a rite of passage. Then the panel of magistrates walked in quickly and sat down. That's when my mouth went dry. For sitting under Her Majesty's emblem was a man in a brown suit with piercing blue eyes.

Alan Prescott.

He glanced down, shuffling paperwork without looking at me. I swore he had a sheepish look on his face. He treated me like a stranger, as if he had no clue whatsoever who I was, and quickly he went through what he needed to say. Likewise, in the dock, I was keen to get out of there, so I stood up and admitted everything. They had me bang to rights, so there was no other choice. Then they rattled through the proceedings and told me I'd have a fine. It was a few hundred quid.

I blew out my cheeks and looked down, hands in pockets. I had no idea where I'd get that kind of money from. Then Alan nodded and court was dismissed. I could sense he wanted me out of there as fast as possible. Still reeling at having seen a paedophile act as a local magistrate, I was getting up to leave when a court official asked me into a side room.

'Mr Connolly, I understand you may have trouble paying this fine,' he began.

'Eh?'

'Yes, you'll need to pay for some of it in instalments, but the court will help you pay for the rest,' he explained.

'Really?' I said, open-mouthed.

I was stunned, but I only questioned it for a split second. Of course, it made sense! If Prescott was a magistrate, he might well be worried about me telling everyone what went on in the home. This must be his way of persuading me to keep my mouth shut.

I mumbled a 'Thanks', not knowing quite what else to say. As sickening as it was that he'd get away with doing this, I couldn't afford the fine anyway. Plus, who would believe a magistrate was a child abuser on the side? I wondered who his friends in high places must be. Were there more abusers like him in positions like this? I reckoned there must be.

As I walked home, a sense of hopelessness overcame me. With nasty pieces of work like Prescott at the top of our justice system, what chance is there of justice? None whatsoever.

*

That night I went out for a few drinks with my mates, mulling over what had happened. I didn't tell them the full story – it was too long to go into – but I told them how fucked up the world was. I longed for distraction, which wasn't hard in a Dagenham pub, so I turned to my favourite one. Violence. That night, I ended up in a scrap in the car park with some herberts from another pub who were kicking off about nothing. I wasn't hurt, as I rarely ended up worse off, and for a few minutes it took my mind off the day's events.

But before too long I found myself in more serious trouble. Our group of twenty-something mates were often joined by an old guy called Steve Hall, a local gangster with a fearsome rep. He always wore loud suits and bowled around the joint like he owned it. He saw himself in a *governor*-type role, but really he was a bully lording it over kids a decade younger than him, extorting money out of some and encouraging others to do his dirty work, whatever that was.

Anyway, I'd been mouthing off about something concerning him to a mutual friend called Budgie, and word got back to him. He decided I needed 'straightening up'. So after a night's drinking, I was told Steve was waiting for me in the pub car park. Now, up until now I'd been in scraps almost every week but nothing too serious, just scraps over someone being a loudmouth or whatever. This was much more serious.

I put down my pint and wandered outside, determined to put a brave face on it. Without a doubt I knew how to handle myself. Thanks to boxing, I knew what punches to throw and what to avoid, so I was intrigued to see what would happen.

'You sure you wanna do this, Jacko?' whispered Psycho Sam as I opened the door.

'I can handle myself,' I shrugged.

Another friend, Charlie Lawrence, looked on with concern. I could tell everyone thought I was facing a good hiding. We'd always heard how gangsters were much more likely to shoot people than use their fists but, with little concern for my life, I thought I'd see what would happen.

I walked outside and quickly spotted Steve waiting near a car. He was much taller than me and didn't hesitate to lay straight in. His body language suggested he expected me to do nothing, but instead I swerved and ducked as he swiped at my ears. He ripped off one earring, then the other, before grabbing my gold necklace, breaking it into pieces.

Fucking hell, I'm losing all my gold here, I thought.

I avoided his next punch, and then he grabbed a pint glass on the ground to try to smash it in my face. But I sidestepped him again and he landed on the ground, the glass cutting his hand. He looked at me with fury as more people gathered outside to watch. So far this hiding wasn't going well for him.

He went for me again, but I just punched him in the side of the face and he went down onto the concrete. The next time he got up he looked a mess, his hand bleeding and his face obviously hurt. He looked around at everyone staring, gobsmacked. Had the *Governor* really been brought down? I had my fists ready in case he came back for more, but he thought better of it and ran off.

'Christ, Jacko, you really showed him what's what,' said Charlie Lawrence. 'Can't believe you did that.'

My heart was burring like an alarm as adrenalin pumped through me. This felt wonderful. If I could see off a bully like Steve Hall, the big guy, I needn't be scared of anyone.

I calmly headed back into the pub to finish my drink before going home. That night, after the adrenalin wore off, I made sure my door was locked and checked the windows a few extra times. The consequence of getting into trouble was fearing people would come after me, especially if I messed with people with reputations like Steve.

I had nothing to worry about, though. A few nights later he asked me to pay for the dry cleaning of his suit, but I told him to fuck off. He lost respect from us lot after that.

This fight proved to me I could do it. I was like an angry dog who'd finally snapped back. Hanging about these pubs was a tough learning experience, but I'd proved my worth. But little did I know what the flipside of this was. Slowly I was morphing from being a frightened little boy, scared of the big, bad world, to being an absolute lunatic who wasn't afraid to jump in headfirst.

*

My reputation as a fighter got around and before long people started to come to me, asking for help to 'sort out' people they felt deserved it. This appealed to me. Not only would I get a buzz out of kicking the shit out of someone, but I also could feel good about it, as it was being handed out to someone who deserved it. Already, whether it was a driver who'd cut me up or some loud drunk picking on his girlfriend, I got stuck in, handing out my form of rough justice. Now I could help out friends who needed it too. I didn't need a psychologist to tell me this was my past catching up with me, that it was my way of knowing that at least some people in life got their just deserts.

Anyway, when my friend, Phil, asked for help, I didn't hesitate to say yes. He was quite a passive character who had been hospitalised by his sister's psycho ex-boyfriend who was stalking her. He'd tried to step in himself but had got a beating, and he'd got no joy going to the police.

'The ex is stalking her at work, he's threatened my family, my sister is on anti-depressants – it's a bloody nightmare, Jacko. Can you step in?' he begged.

'Of course I will,' I said. 'Just give a description of this cunt and his address.'

With everything sorted, I lay in wait for this arsehole to get home after dark, pulled on a balaclava, then pounced on him. Without saying a word, I laid into him, even running his head into his own front door. I never said a word, but he would know exactly why someone had come after him like I had done. That's the thing about people like this; they know they've got it coming one way or another. By the time I'd finished with him he was bleating like a baby lamb on the pavement. He needed treatment in hospital and he never went near his ex again. Job done, as far as I was concerned.

Soon afterwards, though, it was my turn to come off worse. Psycho Sam had told me about a club out of town he loved going to.

'Come with us, Jacko. There's some right tasty birds there.'

So we headed off to the club and moved in on all the hotties, instantly pissing off the local firm who were usually in with a chance.

I always had a knack with the ladies and soon found myself getting a few phone numbers. A couple of the local herberts decided to confront us in the bogs and when they made comments we didn't hold back. Psycho Sam took one, I took the other, and they were spitting blood in the sink by the time we were done. We carried on talking to girls who came over to us and when it was time to leave we had several numbers between us. But as we sauntered out, I spotted a crowd of lads growing quiet as we walked past.

'Sam,' I whispered. 'Run!'

We legged it into a nearby alleyway, but not knowing the area meant we made a fatal mistake. We'd run into a dead end and the two fellas we'd beaten up in the loos had brought their mates with them.

'Fucking hell,' Psycho Sam gasped.

We looked at each other and grimaced. There were about forty blokes, some armed with baseball bats, waiting for us at the alleyway entrance. Knowing we stood no chance, we did what we could and then pretty much accepted the battering. I was smashed in the mouth with a baseball bat, immediately losing all my top row of teeth. All I could do was roll with the punches and hope Psycho Sam survived the kicking like I hoped to do. Thankfully, they could see we'd had enough after a few minutes and they ran off laughing at the damage they'd caused. We helped each other up, covered in blood and bruises. I even managed to smile with teeth missing, blood dripping down my shirt.

'Won't be ringing any of those ladies from tonight any time soon,' I grinned.

*

My life was rapidly splitting into two parts. I was a thug in a pub at night, but I still dreamed of being a professional sportsman by day. After lots of negotiations and finding a suitable training programme, Alan handed me the form to sign, having read it out to me.

'This is it, boy, your professional boxing contract,' he said.

It meant I could get paid for boxing, a dream come true. Yes, the chances of me making it really big were small, we all knew that, including Alan and Tommy. Middleweight was the most popular category and there were loads of amazing boxers, like Nigel Benn and Chris Eubank, who came out of that era. Very few successful amateurs can make that leap into the professional world and succeed. But it did mean I could be a sparring partner for bigger professional boxers, and it meant I could maybe give up roofing for good. Best of all, though, someone believed in me enough to try!

'Thank you,' I said, as I scribbled my name on the form I couldn't read. 'I'll do my best to make this happen.' And I meant it. Learning to fight for a living meant I'd only get better at it, after all.

However hard I tried to look to my future, though, my past from St Leonard's always seemed to have a habit of catching up with me. This time it was the upsetting news about what had happened to a kid from my dorm.

'Have you heard, Paul?' one said in the pub one day. 'Simon's dead.'

'No fucking way!' I replied. The last I'd heard he'd become a father to a baby boy.

'Yeah, it's awful. His veins collapsed or something. His body couldn't take the drugs no more,' my pal told me.

I was stunned. I knew he was a drug addict, but Simon always came across as being smart, confident and somehow in control of his life. Bonkers, considering I also knew that Alan Prescott had groomed him, but he managed to create a character that was very believable.

I stood at the bar, lost in thought. Thinking about that poor lad at the home, the one who always had cash or designer clothes, thanks to the paedophiles. The one who got the swanky caravan on-site and then the three-bedroom house when he moved. He'd been manipulated his whole life until he felt he had no choice but to lose himself in drugs.

Then I thought of the baby boy he'd left behind, fatherless, like poor Simon. He'd tried so hard to tell another story by marrying young, having a baby, committing to a family, but it was still an unhappy ending.

'Poor Simon,' I muttered as my friend changed the subject.

To outsiders it was just a drug addict's death, but I knew full well why he died. I didn't believe it was just heroin that killed him. It was because he could never get over what happened to him at the home.

I couldn't stop thinking about him for days. That legacy of the home was there all the time, even in my sleep and dreams. Was this really what we all had to look forward to? A life of pain and then an early death?

Chapter 14: Close to the Edge

While I looked forward to starting my new professional boxing contract, I continued working on the roofs. After six or seven years on the job, I felt I could do it with my eyes closed and I got cocky with it. The idea of slipping off never bothered me, partly because I was light on my feet and fit, but also because I didn't actually care if I died. It was bravado, but also mixed with a fatalistic view of someone who felt unable to value life deep down.

One afternoon in the summer of 1984, I was working up high on a roof at a caravan site in Upminster. I'd been on the project for three months and knew the layout up high like the back of my hand. I'd undercut local builders by doing a quote without proper scaffolding, so I just relied on ladders on the roof. On this particular day, I jumped up a ladder lying on the roof and it bounced, so I slipped. For a split second, I cycled my legs in the air like Fred Flintstone, before hurtling a full seventy feet down. I had no time to react as I smashed through a glass door at the bottom that had just been taken out by the plasterers. After the initial shock subsided, I heard voices.

'Paul, don't move, stay where you are,' someone said.

'Someone call 999!' said another voice.

My instinct ever since I was a kid has been to run, and right at this moment nothing was going to stop me. So without thinking I ran as fast as my legs would go. It was only when someone screamed at me to stop and caught up with me that I lost my balance, sliding to the ground. Hot liquid like a bath covered my skin, and I saw a young builder throw up his lunch. Only then did I notice my arm was hanging off like a puppet on a string.

'Fucking hell, Paul, you gotta sit down. You're badly hurt. Someone call an ambulance!' said the foreman.

The last thing I recalled was a paramedic's appalled face as he pulled on a rubber glove…

Feeling groggy, I woke up in a hospital bed. As I opened my eyes, my sister Anne was standing over me.

'Paul, you've hurt your arm really badly. Ripped the muscle clean off the shoulder. They want to amputate it,' she said.

My voice emerged just as a croak but I didn't hesitate, however much it hurt.

'Don't let them,' I begged.

I woke the next day with a black priest standing over me. He was doing the cross on my forehead and reading what sounded like the last rites. I felt a profound sense of peace.

I am going home, I thought, feeling like my head was melting into the pillow.

I fell in and out of consciousness over the next few days as the full story of what happened emerged. I'd severed the muscles in my shoulder and lost so much blood the doctors thought I'd die, and now I faced a lifetime of disability. The only saving grace was that Anne had refused to give the doctors permission to chop my arm off, so it was saved and instead I just lost one finger.

'Where's the priest?' I asked one of the nurses.

'What priest?' she asked. I explained I'd seen a black priest giving me the last rites and she looked at me like I was crazy.

'We don't have a black priest working in this hospital,' she said. She claimed I'd dreamt it, but it felt very real to me.

Because of the heavy doses of painkillers I was on, it took days for the news to sink in. I managed to put on a brave face until I saw Alan and Tommy walk in. They sat down beside my bed, faces like the Grim Reaper's.

'You know it's over, Jacko, don't you?' said Alan gently. 'You ain't ever gonna get a boxing licence now.'

Seeing his face, just as fatherly as he was all those years ago when I first stepped into the club with Liam, made the floodgates open. He held me while I sobbed in his arms. He was right. After so many years of dreaming of boxing, I couldn't believe it had all ended like this.

'The only fighting you can do now is unlicensed, and I don't want you getting involved in that game, Jacko,' he said softly. 'But if there is anything else we can help with, we will do.'

I had no Plan B, no other passion in life for me to focus on. All I could do was live in the here and now to try to take my mind off it all. Thankfully, the Dagenham boys helped. They all came up to see me most evenings, using the day room to skin up joints and pass them around. The nurses found visiting hours for me very amusing too. Back then I'd been seeing my building boss's daughter, Jane, but also a lovely Japanese girl I'd chatted up in a club, and another pretty chick called Laura. Trouble was, I wasn't with it enough to work out the timings, so they'd often turn up at my bed at the same time and the nurses were left to try to explain it away.

Despite not being into drugs, I joined the lads for a little toke or two while I thought about what I was going to do for the rest of my life. For the next six weeks, the doctors tried to rehabilitate me as best they could. I had nerve damage and one less finger, which considering the huge injuries was quite miraculous.

Afterwards, I faced months of gruelling physiotherapy to learn to use the bad arm again. This was a difficult time, but to my surprise I found the sessions fascinating. I knew a lot about how the body works through boxing, and my physio taught me even more. I was intrigued by the healing process and spent hours asking questions about how my body was re-learning and how muscles worked. The medical side was a new avenue for me, and after a couple of weeks I started to think what I could do next as a job. If I couldn't train as a boxer, was it possible for me to find something else to get excited about? I racked my brains, unable to think of anything I'd rather do. Until one day I had a session in the hospital gym and slowly realised maybe this could be my way out? If I couldn't box for a living, maybe I could teach other people to keep fit instead and become a gym instructor? Then my mind wandered back to being in my dormitory, with the rows of kids all copying my boxing techniques.

As the idea ran through my mind, I pumped the weights with real energy. Getting fitter was my goal, and as I started to build my body from scratch, maybe I could start a career too. Wiping the sweat from my brow, I chatted to the gym staff and they told me about the basic qualifications I would need to become a personal trainer. It involved lessons and exams, which were totally out of my reach as I couldn't read. But with this time on my hands, perhaps this was a place to start, and so I vowed as I left that hospital gym to find a college that taught adults how to read. Little did I know this was to be one of the hardest things I've ever done.

Chapter 15: Back to Basics

I'd ducked and dived not knowing how to read words for so long that it was second nature. I knew how to blag to people, pretending I could read. At work, when the lads read the newspapers, I'd overhear their conversations and chip in when I could. Or I'd ask friends I trusted the most to read letters sent to me. If I was really stuck I'd frown and say: 'Sorry, I can't read this at the moment. I've forgotten my glasses.'

I hated being so out of control when it came to the world of words, but somehow I had survived. And the more I thought about going back to learning again, the more I panicked. Could the likes of me really sit down behind a desk again? Just thinking about a school environment gave me flashbacks of the Mr Singh and the other thugs, I mean teachers.

But then again, what choice did I have? If you can't read or write, your choices are very limited, and with a bad shoulder now, my options were rapidly becoming even fewer. Then what? End up like the other kids who turned to crime? Or depressed and suicidal? Once again Auntie Coral's prophecies were coming dangerously close. No. I had to face my demons and learn everything I should have learned twenty years earlier. It was the only chance I had.

After making some enquiries I found a college that did classes for illiterate adults. It was funded by the government, the irony being that at last the government was providing a much-needed organised service, unlike the care system. So I signed up, asking the college staff to fill in the forms for me.

The first day felt a million times worse than being back at school. I wanted to hide my face with shame. This time I was sitting in a room with adults who clearly had learning difficulties and this shattered any sense of self-worth again, as the teachers spoke to us all like we were idiots. I knew I wasn't daft, but deep down I questioned who I really was, especially without boxing. It was impossible to act like Jack the Lad in a place like this.

I left on the first day not knowing whether I could stick it out. But I knew I had to. I had seen a qualification I needed to start a career as a personal trainer, and being able to read was the only way I could get the piece of paper. So I made sure I didn't miss a single

lesson. Unlike when I was at school, I did my homework, until –
painfully slowly – letters on a page made sense.

One teacher, Grace, encouraged me with real patience and
kindness. She sat with me for hour after hour, going over
everything slowly and encouraging me every time I made progress.
Grace taught me what a good teacher is like, because I'd never had
one before. By being positive, calm and encouraging, she helped
my abilities to slowly grow. When I think back to the bullies who
enjoyed caning us kids, I still feel angry. They're a disgrace to the
profession.

Over the next two long years I worked on rebuilding my body
and re-educating my brain. One was easier than the other, as I
struggled so much with learning to read. It didn't come naturally,
and often my frustration boiled into anger. But Grace was such a
positive influence, I found myself sticking it out.

Meanwhile I needed to earn some money, so the coaches were
true to their word and found me a job in a spit-and-sawdust gym
run by two ex-wrestlers called Derek and Percy. Luckily, just before
the accident I'd finally passed my driving test, so I could also take
up their offer of minicabbing work. They even provided me with a
car with a special steering wheel.

Finally, I had access to one my main sources of distraction again:
women. Although women are often seen as the shyer sex, that's not
my experience as when I started driving it wasn't just paying
passengers I was picking up. With my thick dark hair, Irish blue
eyes and easy banter, I often got chatted up, and more often than
not I got asked inside for a coffee after the fare was sorted.
Sometimes I'd arrange to meet several girls in a night after
knocking off my shift. The only thing I had to remember was their
house or flat number. On the odd occasion I'd get it wrong and
end up ringing the doorbell of some horny girl's sleeping next-door
neighbour!

*

While working by day in the gym, I met loads of doormen who
pumped iron to beef themselves up. Through more contacts of my
coaches, I started to get offers to mind the doors of some of the
most notorious clubs in Essex and East London.

'It's a tough gig,' I was warned. 'There's often trouble, but it's good money.'

That sounded like a dream job to me. The chance of teaching badly behaved punters a lesson *and* getting paid for it? When did I start? Now I finally had my second favourite distraction back again: access to violence.

The first club I worked at was the Princess Alice in Forest Gate. This place was like something out of the Wild West. It was long before door security became licensed, so the rules were: there are no rules. Punters were a melting pot of different cultures – Scottish, Irish, Gypsies, Africans – many of them specifically looking for trouble. Every night it wasn't a question of 'if' there would be violence, it was a case of 'when' it would kick off.

If I'd handed in a CV outlining my personality for this job, anyone would have been able to tell I was completely unsuitable for it. With a hair-trigger temper, a love of fighting and an insatiable need to punish those who 'deserved it', I should never have been allowed anywhere near a door.

When arriving on the first night, I soon realised I was by far the shortest doorman there. But my new colleagues realised I made up for this with attitude. Those first few nights, punters liked to start with me, thinking they'd take down the smallest doorman, but they always got a shock when my fists met their faces with such speed and precision that they'd instantly regret it. I got on much better with my colleagues, however, and earned a nickname, 'Fingers', thanks to my missing one.

Often the punters took bets on who could knock down a doorman first or who could get their gun inside. We often searched the queue and had to take weapons off people. Halfway through the night, police officers would come in and confiscate what we had in our 'tool chest', as they knew they'd find something. As I got ready for work every night I never knew what was going to happen or what fight I'd be in next, so of course I loved it.

Inevitably, one night things went too far and I got quite badly hurt after confiscating a gangster's gun. After the club had closed, he waited in the shadows for me and launched at me with a screwdriver. I felt him use a tool, but I wasn't sure what it was, so I just went for him afterwards. As I punched him I felt the warmth spreading over my shirt and I touched my stomach, only to realise I'd been stabbed. I went for him after that still, leaving him battered and bloodied on the ground.

When the police arrived, they took one look at me and then at him. He was lying on the ground, wincing, as his mates tried to get him to stand up, while I was standing over him, bleeding like a stuck pig from the wound in my side.

'You can go,' the police said. 'We can see he's harmed you too.'

Talk about police acting as judge and jury, but I was happy with this verdict so I politely thanked them and went home. The following night I turned up at work with a clean shirt on like it had never happened.

Over the next year or so, I worked in clubs all over the Essex and East London areas. Working at one in the East End, I'll call Charlie's, was like having a holiday in comparison to some of the Essex clubs, because the punters were a higher-class clientele and not as keen on violence. It made nights boring for me at times, though.

Through my door work, I gained a reputation as someone who didn't give a shit and was like a dog unleashed when attacked, but someone who was also trustworthy and knew right from wrong. So when, through my associates, I got offered the chance to act as a minicab driver and a minder at the same time for big bucks, I jumped at the chance. I had no idea how closely all the worlds interlinked, how working on a posh club door could lead you to these people, but there were some seriously rich high-profile clients, from celebrities to politicians to rich gangsters, all knocking about in the same world. And now I'd become part of it.

One of my jobs, alongside a couple of the other trusted guys, was to look after super-rich Arabs when they came over here. Back home, these princes were living in a strict society where they were not allowed to drink, have casual sex, take drugs or go clubbing, so coming over to London was like being in a giant playground. Often the first thing they wanted to do was to get laid. But instead of quietly getting a couple of nice girls to go back to their hotel, they'd insist on going out to clubs and finding someone to pull. It was all about their egos, wanting someone to want them. Fair enough, you might think, except it caused us huge headaches.

Often, when the Arabs arrived at a club with a big fanfare to chat up the birds, it would piss off the local herberts. At the end of the day, these princes were more likely to get a bullet in the back of the head than a shag from a girl. Fights would break out all the time and we'd have to mop it all up. Soon, every time the call came to look after some super-rich Arab we'd all eye-roll and say, 'Not the fucking Arabs again!'

But the money was amazing and I was good at my job. When more work came my way, I didn't say no, even if it involved more risk. I started to help gangsters with their families, as many had wives as well as girlfriends. Often I'd drive them from A to B, acting as a driver and a minder.

By now I'd recovered my full fitness and was built like a tank, so what I lacked in size I made up for in stature. Along with my body, my reputation for violence had grown too, so suddenly I was being offered jobs that were riskier and more dangerous by gangsters who meant business.

*

Proper gangsters stay under the radar, unlike all the big hitters that get films and books done about them. This particular gangster family were one of the most powerful in East London in the 1980s and they owned several brothels, stretching from East London to Essex. Six of them were on one long road.

First of all I got a call, asking me to mind a few brothels or 'saunas', some fancy ones near Regent Street that boasted a celebrity and posh clientele, including super-famous politicians.

'You're perfect for this, Fingers. You can be a nasty nutter, but you've got morals. Know what I mean?' this associate said.

'Yeah,' I agreed. Pretending I did.

It cost £500 just to get inside one of these places and then you had to sit, chat to the girls to explain what you wanted and then pay more accordingly. It was our job to make sure nothing happened to the girls, who had cameras in their rooms so we watched from outside. If they ever hit their panic buttons, we had to jump in there and save them. To say this job was an eye-opener is an understatement.

The higher up the chain the client was, the more degrading the sex required it seemed. I saw politicians, gagged and dressed as babies, being fucked up the arse with a dildo, something we laughed at but deep down I felt a bit disturbed by.

It took all sorts. There was a noticeable preference from certain Indian gentlemen for ladies to defecate on them. I'll never forget the Indian guy who had one long, small fingernail in order to extract poo from one of the girl's bottoms as he finished off. Or the prostitute who told us she'd made sure she'd eaten a curry the night before her appointment with a dignitary who'd booked a sex-and-poo session.

'Got to make sure it slips out easily,' she explained. Ugh! Dirty fucking cow.

I dreaded watching what some punters insisted on having done to them, especially the asphyxiation-style sex or the posh gits that liked to jack up on heroin before a bonk. I even had a word with management about my fears of an accidental death.

'You know if someone dies here the whole joint will be investigated,' I said. But they shrugged their shoulders and insisted that what punters wanted they got. And to think some rich people were paying as much as a monkey for a night in this gaff.

Then the phone rang again for another job. This time it was for a woman who had been stalked by her ex-boyfriend. All the gangsters had wives but also several girlfriends, and this lady was being hassled by an ex where she lived with her teenage daughter. He sounded like a right lunatic, so I was asked to sleep over at her house to protect her. It wasn't expected he'd show up, but in case he did I would be ready, alongside another minder, to sort him out. I slept tooled up, like I did every night anyway, on her sofa. Night after peaceful night nothing happened, until one night I woke up to find someone standing over me with a knife. I leapt up just as he stabbed me in the side.

'Fuck!' I screamed as the other minder jumped on him. We looked up to see this geezer had managed to pop off the entire patio door and just walk in.

Not willing to give him any more chances, I went full force, battering him, as my friend laid into him even more enthusiastically. Within seconds, blood splattered up all the orange-painted walls and coated the carpet like paint as my bouncer mate carried on.

'He's had enough,' I yelled above the sound of the woman and her daughter screaming outside the living-room door.

The guy was on the floor, semi-conscious, and his face unrecognisable with blood. I feared his skull had been broken at the very least. As the other minder laid off, he crawled away, back through the patio doors. Then he staggered up and started running – for his life, I imagine he thought.

The room we were standing in looked like a psycho killer had visited, but there was no time to clean up. We decided to look for him to make sure he wasn't going to bring back a gang to finish us off. We also knew if he decided to press charges we were fucked. We ran outside the back of the house and into a churchyard, following a trail of blood. But after fifteen minutes of searching behind gravestones, we found nothing. He had vanished.

The lady of the house rang her gangster associate and I went home to clean up. After barely sleeping that night I returned to the house the next day, where I had the shock of my life. The room had already been redecorated completely. The orange walls were now green, a new carpet was laid and all new settees were arranged around the room. It was like a different house.

'They even took down the plastering to the brickwork so forensics would never stand a chance,' said the other minder. The speed of it being done, let alone the cost of it, was staggering. But I'd learned if a gangster wants to get something done, they get it done.

Anyway, after doing a couple of jobs I began to worry about being involved with such events. Although I never did anything that was more than self-defence, I was at risk of being embroiled in something that truly could get out of control. But my name was out there now, amongst people who wanted someone to trust to hand out justice or protect those who needed it. And if nothing else, I was trustworthy.

The next time, instead of being a minder, I was asked to act as a vigilante. Our associate explained that a violent gang of Africans were turning up out of the blue, targeting brothels and raping the girls.

'They use surprise tactics, coming out of nowhere. They've got to be stopped,' he said.

I was appalled to hear about this, as we felt protective over these women. Many of them were lovely girls. In my view it was untrue that all prostitutes were desperate drug addicts. Most of them earned £500 a night or more and were well looked after. Also, I knew a lot of the girls came from the care system too. One or two even offered us freebies when it was quiet, something I never took them up on as I was control freak and terrified of contracting something. Funnily enough, they'd get offended when we turned them down.

Now this gang was threatening not only the lives of the girls but also the gangsters' livelihoods. The remit was: 'Get as nasty as you want and don't just *hurt* them, *proper hurt* them.' I'd been approached along with two other minders, Phil and Vince, as we all had reputation for violence.

Happy as always to see justice being meted out, I couldn't wait to get stuck in, so we all turned up for work ten days in a row. The idea was to wait upstairs for them and then clobber whoever came in. But nothing happened. I'd just started to wonder if they'd stopped the attacks, when we heard a racket downstairs. The door was being kicked in.

We jumped into position, me by the top of the stairs with a baseball bat. Immediately the girls started screaming and their clients ran naked from the rooms, wondering what the hell was happening.

'You ready?' Vince yelled at me as I stood behind a door. He was built like a brick shit house and was someone I would never want to mess with.

'You bet,' I yelled back, winking at Phil, who stood on the other side.

We didn't have a game plan except to teach this gang a lesson, so when five men came steaming up the stairs there was no time to hesitate.

As the first one, a big black man, reached the top I swung my bat as hard as I could into his face. He instantly fell backwards, on top of the others, who all tumbled like dominos. They landed in a pile at the foot of the stairs in the small hallway, the security door closing neatly behind them, so they were trapped. Trouble was, so were we. And now we had to deal with this human tower of thugs, all struggling to get up again.

'Fuck!' cried Vince, pulling out his gun.

He ran downstairs and started grabbing at their legs. Then, to my horror, he fired the gun at point-blank range into kneecaps. Giving someone a 'kneecapping' is a classic gangster way of teaching them a lesson, but I'd never seen it happen before. The men were screaming as Vince grappled with the ends of their trousers, pulling them towards him so he could take aim. Blood and pieces of bone squirted up the walls and splattered our faces so we looked like something out of a horror film.

'Vince!' I screamed as the men writhed in agony. My heart was racing – I feared bullets ricocheting off the walls as we were in such a small space. 'Let's go!' I yelled.

Vince and Phil took one last look at the carnage as we turned to escape. By now the whole house was full of people screaming with fear as I scoured for somewhere to escape from.

'Oi, you're last, you fat cunt. If you go first none of us are getting out,' I said.

'Vince, get the fuck up here. I've found a way out,' I cried, opening a window. I reached outside to feel for the drainpipe on the wall. It wobbled but would have to do. Vince tried to get out first, but I stopped him.

I slid down it, then Phil came and then lastly Vince, who predictably pulled the whole thing off.

The sight of him picking himself up from the ground made us all laugh, until we heard sirens growing louder.

'Let's go!' I yelled.

We leapt into a car parked behind the brothel and tore off down the road, all three of us looking like we'd been in the movie *Carrie*. We drove at breakneck speed to Epping Forest, where we tore off our clothes and set fire to them, before burying the gun. Then we dropped Phil off at his place, before pulling in at Vince's.

Now, what I *should* have done was ask to borrow clothing from Vince, even if he was five sizes bigger than me, but without thinking I just got back in the car to drive home. This meant driving home along busy A-roads stark-bollock naked with my face smeared with blood. Talk about being conspicuous! Thankfully, nobody noticed me and I got home and went straight to my sink to wash.

Only afterwards did I think of all the rookie mistakes we'd made and how fortunate we'd been not getting caught. I don't think the police were ever called for this incident, and if they were, no investigation was made. Thankfully, as nasty as it had been, the Africans never attacked the brothels again.

We'd done such a good job, we got paid a handsome bonus for our work and it wasn't long before I was asked to do another one. But by now I was worrying about being part of this underworld. I'd been building up a personal training business and my gangster work was at odds with what I was trying to achieve in my work life: earn a decent, law-abiding living.

Chapter 16: A Double Life

Things were spinning out of control, as the two Pauls I battled with were emerging as very different characters. By night I was getting involved in street violence, while by day I was a model student, struggling with my reading demons and a sense of imposter syndrome.

As soon as I could read well enough to understand the basics, I signed up for a Fitness for Industry certificate in a bid to make the first step towards becoming a personal trainer. The course was intense and one of my biggest challenges. We had to attend lectures all day and then we had around six hours' homework at night. I stayed at a hotel in Hammersmith near where the course was being held so I wasn't late in the morning.

Luckily, I managed to team up with a girl student. She was a right swot who knew the theory, so while she helped me with that, I helped her with the practical side of things, which she was shit at. For the first time in my life I had a girl in my bedroom who I wasn't shagging. Although, I admit, that never stopped me from trying it on with her.

'Sure you don't wanna try some push-ups on the bed?' I teased her.

She rolled her eyes and tapped the books. 'We're here to study. No time for any of that, Paul.'

I was glad in the end, as she was right: we needed to work if we were going to pass, especially me, as I still struggled with spelling beyond simple words. It wasn't easy, but thanks to my knowledge of fitness and physiology, I managed to pass. The examiner did say if I'd been judged on spelling I'd have failed, but I didn't care. As long as I had the piece of paper I could take my next step, which was to do other courses and then carry on working at the gym. I was twenty-seven years old and finally had a qualification to my name.

While I worked hard behind the scenes, earning all my stripes in the gym world, on the streets my nasty streak was getting out of control. Instead of growing out of my anger, I was finding it was steadily getting worse and by my late twenties I was more confident than ever in being able to handle myself. Trouble was, it was out of all proportion to what was happening. I actively looked for ways to teach people who I decided deserved it a lesson, and nowhere was I more triggered than when out driving my car.

I was always excessively polite as a driver, but then as soon as someone crossed me or did something I perceived to be out of order, I'd go nuts. For example, while coming home one day I gave way to a Merc whose driver gave me the finger as he went past, so I chased him for a few miles before he pulled off into a hotel car park. He thought he'd lost me but I followed him, and after a few laps of the car park he tried to pull off onto the M25. There, he got stuck in traffic. So, undeterred by the five lanes of stationary cars, I jumped out to pull him out of the car and give him what for. After I finished hitting him, I heard screaming from the passenger seat and looked over to see his wife. I leaned into his car and handed her my phone number written down.

'If you want a proper fuck, give me a ring,' I suggested. 'Because clearly you're not getting a proper fuck from your husband.'

This cockiness was only ever going to get me into trouble and after I came down from my adrenalin high I realised how stupid I'd been. Leaving my phone number like that was an open invitation for the police to come and get me.

Another time I was driving down a country lane in the dark with a white van right up my backside. I stopped and he pulled over to have a go. But while the mug was thinking he'd get away with it, I reached into his open window, pulled out his ignition keys and threw them into the pitch-black forest. All the time I was thinking: *Those cunts won't get away with it. And if I don't sort them out, who will?*

Nothing stopped my temper when it came to road rage, even a van full of five guys. They were giving me all that at some lights, so I raced them and we ended up pulling over. I had a metal cosh in the car, so I pulled that out and smashed up their front window. They all ran off from what they saw as a psycho. Which was me.

It wasn't long before the dark side of this life I was leading came into full focus, when two doormen I knew were killed on the job. One of them was Chrissie, a big bear of a fella with a good heart, who worked the door at a club I'll call Jungle. This place was mental, a big old movie theatre that needed fifty doormen to manage it as it attracted trouble like bees to honey. I was the only white bouncer among all the black fellas, and often they would tease me, saying I might as well have a target on my head. Of course, knowing how dangerous this place was gave me a buzz like no other. I loved getting ready for work, wondering how it would kick off and what I'd be involved in.

But then things took a turn for the worse. One night, a night I wasn't booked to work there, a drug dealer upset with a promoter stuck a gun in the doorway and fired, injuring more than ten people and killing poor Chrissie. The bullet ricocheted off his elbow and went behind his bulletproof vest and straight into his heart. It was terribly bad luck.

Another doorman I knew got shot in the heart in a club in Stratford. With clubs teeming with shady characters and drug dealers, they were very dangerous places to be. But the constant adrenalin of not knowing if I'd make it through a night alive meant I had no need for drugs, aside from the very occasional line of coke to keep me awake and the odd drink.

Meanwhile, in daylight hours I was rapidly gaining a reputation as someone who was passionate about fitness, especially using boxing moves whilst training. Boxing is one of the best ways of keeping fit, as it uses so many muscle groups and really improves your aerobic fitness fast. It was natural for me to teach people what I knew best.

With a sprig of hope that life was moving forwards at last, it was all the more upsetting to hear what had happened to another boy from my dormitory. Mark Byrnes had driven his car off Beachy Head and killed himself, someone who knew him told me. So that was two of the boys I lived with for years cut down in their prime – although I wondered if it was possible for anyone from St Leonard's to reach their 'prime'.

Mark had left the home late, like me, and I don't think he'd managed very well at all outside of St Leonard's. I knew he'd been raped from a young age, and he was never the brightest spark. He'd even attempted a life of crime by holding up post offices at gunpoint and then making his escape in a pre-ordered taxi waiting outside. Of course, he quickly got caught. None of this surprised me, as he couldn't read either. He stood no chance getting an ordinary job, let alone dealing with all of his emotional problems. The poor bastard probably felt he had nothing to live for.

That was the thing about leaving a care home: you were left with nothing. No skills, no support, no basic knowledge of how life works. It meant so many just ended up in prison or dead. Auntie Coral was right in that respect, and the fear never left me that this would eventually be my destiny too.

Although financially things were going well, occasionally an offer came along from the underworld that was too good to turn down. So one day when I was approached to do an unlicensed fight, I said yes. This was something I'd never considered before, since Alan had warned me off, but in one night I could earn thousands, money that could go towards the new gym courses I needed to further my career.

The venue was a warehouse on an old industrial estate in Beckton. Once everyone was inside, the gate would be chained shut to keep punters in and the Old Bill out. There were no changing rooms, so I got changed in the car and then wandered in – only to find a baying mob, all taking bets on who was going to win.

'What are the odds like?' I asked someone.

'Against you!' he laughed.

I was stunned to see such a big crowd, many of them local gangsters who were all backing the other fighter. I had no idea who this geezer was, but I knew I'd give it my best shot. Thankfully I had friends who'd come to support me too.

As I wrapped up my hands before putting my gloves on, it occurred to me there was no referee checking them. *I could easily have slipped a knuckleduster into this,* I thought, before wondering if my opponent would be doing exactly that.

There was no doctor on-site either, just a dodgy pharmacist who was on hand for the worst-case scenario. There was also no proper ring. It was just a square of land cleared for two men to fight it out. These were the days before cage fighting or mixed martial arts; it was just a matter of the fighters using whatever techniques they liked, including all the dirty tricks they could think of.

For all my bravado, the moment I clapped eyes on my opponent I felt my insides clench. He was very tall and broad, and he was practising kicks like a professional kick boxer. *Fucking hell,* I thought as he high-kicked the air. *If he lands one on my head, I'll die.* And I knew full well the only time a referee in an unlicensed fight does interfere is if you *are* going to die.

But there was no time to think too much as the crowd roared for it to begin. I managed a few quick punches, swerving a couple of his kicks, as he paced around. Then he swiftly moved to one side of the ring, looking as if he planned to kick me.

He'll never reach me from there... was my last thought before suddenly, like flash lightning, he kicked me in the face.

Shit, I thought. I'd completely underestimated this geezer.

The volume of the crowd was deafening as I managed to roll away from under him on the floor. The only ways to stop your opponent were either tapping your hand on the floor or getting up, so I got up. Quickly, I realised my lack of grappling and wrestling skills meant I needed to strike hard with punches, and I put my full weight behind all of them.

Bam, bam, bam.

Only then did I spot something in his eyes. Fear. I knew I had a chance now, as I honestly could have fought to the death, and when your opponent recognises that in you, you've won.

On and on I punched, determined to see him tapping that floor. He kept getting up, so I hooked him from below, smashing my fist into his ribs. The twist of pain on his face was what I was looking for. *I've proper hurt you,* I thought as he went down.

Each round was supposed to be five minutes, but there was no way we were going to last that long. He managed to stand up again, but with his ribs broken, my previously high-kicking friend couldn't lift his legs. So he gave up, defeated.

Grinning, I stood up, arms raised, the victor! But my elation didn't last long as the cheering stopped. Here I was some unknown entity who'd beaten one of the best guys. I didn't know what to do. Then my mates pulled me aside.

'We're having a party tonight, Jacko,' one said.

After my win I should have walked away from unlicensed fighting then and there, but I went on to fight several more times.

With so much anger inside me, the temptation was too great. Until the day I came up against an opponent who taught me a lesson.

When I stepped into the ring that time, I knew I faced a big challenge. I'd been put up against big guys before, but this geezer must have been twenty-three stones or more.

I can't let this fat cunt get me on the floor or I'm finished, was my first thought.

We sparred for a bit, him coming off worse, but he was a good grappler and soon he had me down and in a headlock.

'You need to tap out,' he growled at me, as my whole body shook under the weight of him.

'Nah, I ain't tapping!' I cried.

'You need to tap!' he screamed.

'I said: I AIN'T tapping!' I replied.

Finding strength from somewhere, I managed to throw him off. But soon enough he had me back down again, having punched me in the face several times.

'You'd better tap,' he growled again. 'Or I'll put you to sleep!'

I knew just one movement would cut off my air supply and I'd end up unconscious, but even then I couldn't bring myself to do it.

'I. Ain't. Tapping,' I said through gritted teeth as he swivelled my arm into a position above me, over his elbow.

I knew what was coming next and even then I couldn't bring myself to give in. I closed my eyes as a sickening crack like a broken twig followed. The cunt had just broken my arm. I lurched over to my side, game over. The crowd's yelling was deafening as I got carried out the door. My eye socket was a mess, my nose was broken and my jaw felt shattered. Someone medical cast a quick, unsympathetic eye over me, and I was ushered away to my next stop, the local hospital.

Those injuries took several months to heal and meant taking time off work, so I knocked the unlicensed fights on the head after that.

*

Despite my underground lifestyle, on the outside my career was going great guns. By the late 1980s, I was being promoted within gyms in Essex, and then my big break came along. I spotted an advert for a free weights manager at The Barbican, a fancy gym in London, so I applied. This was the go-to place for celebrities from both sides of the pond, with stars like Jodie Foster, Charles Dance, Nigel Benn and even Superman, Christopher Reeve, working out there. Probably helped by my Irish gift of the gab, I did well in the interview and beat off thirty other instructors to get offered the job.

On my first day, imposter syndrome set in because I couldn't believe the likes of me would be hobnobbing with celebrities and stars. Me, Paul Connolly, a.k.a. Jacko, who'd been told from the age of eight that he'd never amount to anything, working with high-class clients, lawyers, company directors and the like? It didn't seem possible!

Yet it was, and I did it, fitting in with my easy banter and ability to focus on the job. At the gym my anger issues and lack of education didn't matter, because I could show people how to get fit and that was all they wanted to know. All my boxing skills came into play as I taught clients how being a boxer isn't just about throwing punches and your weight around, it's about using your body's agility and strength and working out different muscle groups. I found people loved learning to box, and of course throwing punches is a good stress reliever.

Around this time I was to bump into a man who became an important friend in my life. Up until now my best mates had been doormen and Dagenham boys, thugs and rough diamonds among them, but I couldn't call any of them role models, except for the older boxing coaches. Anyway, in my day job I bumped into Ian Mecklenburgh, who was designing a computer system in an Essex gym. We were like chalk and cheese. He was the educated, posh, nice guy. I was the thug from the wrong side of the tracks, but who wanted to better himself. Following some banter, we realised we lived around the corner from each other and decided to hook up for a drink. Both of us were bachelors and we joined forces to have fun together. The more I got to know Ian, the more I admired him. He was from a decent family and had been brought up with a definite sense of right from wrong. He was dead keen to hear about my coaching and boxing work. He gave me the confidence to think I could push things further too. I found myself looking forward to seeing him, as I wanted some of his solid personality to rub off on me.

One day we were having a few drinks in a bar when a girl I fancied wandered past. I gave her a little look, but her boyfriend took exception to that and started on me. I stood up to confront him, but Ian placed a hand on my arm just before I kicked things off.

'What are you doing, Paul?' he said quietly. 'There's no need for it.'

'What?' I cried. 'What do you mean?'

'I mean you're escalating the situation, making it worse, and there's no need for it. The guy's a prick. Let him rant, then ignore him,' Ian said.

Nobody had ever stepped in and said this quite so simply before. Incredible as it sounds, I always met aggression head on with aggression and I'd never imagined it could work any other way. So, against all my instincts, I let the matter go and the guy soon walked off. Ian and I enjoyed the drink and nobody got hurt. Sounds incredible, but this was one of the first times I realised how off-key my behaviour was. For so many years I'd only ever sorted out altercations with confrontation – usually fists.

'I know it seems stupid, but I'm not sure how to sort out disagreements without getting into a fight,' I admitted at the end of the night. 'It's like, that's all I know to do.'

'It's just a different way of approaching situations,' Ian replied. 'You can do it, Paul.'

*

As I was teaching the general public, I had to develop new exercises that were gentler than how a real athlete would train, and within weeks I found I had accidentally invented a new way to keep fit that was fun and effective. I talked to Ian about it and we decided to go into business together by trademarking the name *Boxerobics™*. This was when aerobics had had its heyday, so now it was time for a new exercise to take its place.

Word quickly spread about the new, funky classes and soon I couldn't teach enough of them. I even started taking money from clubs as I was a bona fide instructor with a name for himself and I was also training their trainers. Suddenly, I no longer had to rely on door work and was really doing okay.

Then something else happened that I could never have anticipated. Journalists got wind of *Boxerobics™* and asked to interview me for magazines like *Time Out* and *Health*. Suddenly I was hailed as one of the first qualified personal trainers who could teach *Boxerobics™*. Paul Connolly was hot property!

All the attention led to the production company of supermodel Elle McPherson approaching me to help make a fitness video in Miami. I jumped at the chance, especially as it involved a trip to the States, a mind-blowing experience for someone who had hardly travelled. I never met Elle, but after giving advice on her video I was promised a credit.

Annoyingly, the production company, Pickwick Pictures, didn't stick to their part of the deal and my name was left off the DVD cover. I was screwed, and when they asked me to do it again, I refused. Looking back, I should have sought legal representation at the time, but I never did.

Still, I had more press than ever, even appearing in papers my old workmates read like *The Sun*. Next, TV researchers rang to ask me to appear on their shows. So one morning I found myself on *The Big Breakfast* being interviewed by Paula Yates, who joined in with my little exercise routine for a week.

'Introduced as an ex-amateur-boxing champion, qualified fitness instructor and the top, top *Boxerobics™* expert…' she said. 'Paul Connolly!'

I should have been nervous as hell doing live TV, but as always my blagging side kicked in and I just focused on the task in hand.

'It's good for releasing aggression, for releasing stress,' I explained to Paula, showing off the moves.

She joined in and we had a right laugh on and off camera. Paula was lovely and arrived on set every morning at five a.m. looking like she'd been out partying all night, only to emerge an hour later looking every inch the star. She found it very amusing to pinch my bum when she could get away with it too. Everyone took the piss out of me and I loved it. I wore tiny little shorts, as they were the fashion back then.

'Your dick is going to fall out of them!' Paula laughed.

I met so many stars that week, including Michael Hutchence, Robin Williams and Julie Walters. Of course, I was most excited to meet Zig and Zag, the puppets – well, the Irish guys who had their hands up their arses, but you know what I mean. I had a thing for Gaby Roslin, so was a bit disappointed to see that when the cameras weren't pointing in her direction her smile soon disappeared. Chris Evans was more down to earth, though. When I was standing in his way, he edged past me saying, ''Scuse me, star coming through,' proving he had a sense of humour. All of them hung out in the green room with us to eat bacon rolls too.

This TV role led to others, including spots on *Good Morning with Anne and Nick*, a session with Anna Walker on The Ross King show, the late-night sports programme *Under the Moon* and *The Word*.

The whirlwind of attention made me feel like a success for the first time in my life, even if it wasn't a sensation I could hold on to. Deep down I was still the kid from the children's home. I even found myself wondering if the likes of Auntie Coral and Bill Starling had spotted me on TV. What would they think? That despite everything I'd proved Auntie Coral wrong? I wasn't dead or in prison, I was on the telly! Would they even be bothered if they did know? Other people did spot me, however, like my brother, Declan, who got back in touch.

'Alright, Paul. I saw you on telly the other day,' he said on the phone. 'Fancy meeting up?'

I wasn't sure. Although he was my brother, we were still pretty much estranged. Declan lived on a council estate in Barking and I knew he'd struggled with his past since leaving care. I didn't want to cut him off, but I couldn't see us being friends.

'My schedule is pretty hectic…' I began, but he cut in.

'Listen,' he said. '*The Big Breakfast* is filmed near Archer House, which is where social services kept all our files from our years in care. I'm going down to read them, if you want to join me?'

Part of me didn't. Why would I want to go through all that again? Reading words written by the likes of Starling and Coral?

What would I gain from it? But then the bigger part of me was curious. There were so many blanks and questions about my past; it made sense to find out.

'Okay then,' I agreed. 'Let's do it.'

So after filming one day, I met Declan outside Archer House. Inside, we were led to a private room, with a counsellor on hand in case we got upset. As I was handed the file, I was struck by how thick it was. Twelve years is a long time. People get less for murder. I opened it tentatively. The first thing I read was the date of birth on my birth certificate.

'Hang on,' I said to the counsellor woman. 'Is this right?'

The counsellor nodded her head. 'All dates of birth in the files are correct,' she said.

'But it says here I was born on August the twenty-second. I spent my whole life being told it was August the second!' I cried.

She gave me a look and frowned. 'It's correct,' she said. 'You must have been told wrongly as a child then.'

I sat back in my chair, blown away. I knew my social worker and the staff at St Leonard's were neglectful, but not even bothering to know a child's proper birthday? It was unbelievable!

I continued to flick through the pages.

Paul is a troubled character… Paul wets the bed… Paul is a very violent little boy… Paul is continually in fights…

On and on it went, all in that bastard Bill Starling's scrawly hand. Then Declan started giggling.

'Hey, look at this, Paul,' he said, reading from his file. 'Says here: "Declan is a very troubled child who wears women's clothing. We believe he is a cross-dresser and think he's a homosexual!"'

'What?' I laughed. 'You?' By now Declan was married with three kids of his own.

'Yeah, they're questioning my sexuality when I'm just a little kid who probably wore something for a joke.'

'Ha ha, well, when you think these files were written by a bunch of paedos, I suppose it makes sense!' I roared.

We both fell about in our chairs, laughing our heads off.

The counsellor lady started tutting; she couldn't understand where the humour was. But the fact was, if we didn't find black humour in the sadness, we'd have sat and cried.

I just closed the file in the end, having read enough. It wasn't going to change anything of the past. So much of it I was trying so hard to block out. Bloody awful times.

Shortly after this, Matty got in touch out of the blue too and invited me over to his house. He was living in Stoke Newington, and when I arrived at his three-storey place I was bowled over. He'd really done all right for himself, running his own business and married with kids too. We still felt like strangers, but seeing him gave me hope it was possible for a Connolly to do well in life. I sensed too he was different to my other brothers. He never felt sorry for himself or acted like a victim, which is sadly the mentality for a lot of adults who lived in care homes as kids. We stayed in touch, but back then I never felt like there was a bond there. We Connollys were all eager to forget where we came from, I think.

Chapter 17: Confronting Demons

I was asked to open classes at Danceworks on Oxford Street, one of the most famous studios in London, and was thrilled to accept the offer. Business was booming!

For the first time in my life I'd become secure financially, making enough to buy my first home. I paid cash for a two-bedroom railway cottage near Brentwood station with a small garden. I specifically chose a house on a corner plot of land because it meant I could see in all directions. This was because although on the outside I was a successful personal trainer, on the inside I was still a paranoid wreck. Nothing I did managed to help me relax. I slept with every tool going – knives, a baseball bat, a gas cylinder, a knuckle duster on and a cosh by my bed. My paranoia was so bad I wouldn't dare to sleep in the same room every night. I would alternate between my bedroom, the small back room and then the living room.

There was no specific thing I was afraid of. I didn't fear the people I worked with or for. Nobody knew where I lived and, even if they did, I didn't have a vendetta against me as far as I knew. No. My brain was still wired to feel fear every single day, regardless of how safe life was. The legacy from St Leonard's.

I got several offers to mind doors as well and, despite trying to give it up, the lure of money and the prospect of the fights made the offers too good to turn down and so my double life continued. During the week I was doing all kinds of celebrity work, but at the weekend I was minding doors, gunning for a fight. Only very occasionally did my two lives collide and I'd get recognised as That Guy Off the Telly. I could be knocking some troublemaker's teeth out when he'd look up and say, 'Aren't you that trainer bloke?' So I'd have to hit him harder so he couldn't speak.

It never occurred to me I could get found out – or probably, subconsciously, it did, but I buried it.

Looking back, I see my need for the violence was bordering on obsessive. If I couldn't sleep, I thought nothing of leaving the house in the middle of the night, all tooled up, to go looking for trouble. I never wanted to cause it; I just wanted to save someone from being hurt. On these occasions, my destination wasn't nightclubs or high streets at chucking out time. I went to dark, lonely country lanes or woods, where I imagined horrible men lying in wait, maybe for a woman or an unsuspecting passer-by. I'd walk for miles, specifically hoping I'd find someone who was obviously up to no good, just so I could set about them legitimately and teach them a lesson. Somewhere deep down, the older, stronger kid still wanted to keep the bullies at bay, as crazy as that sounds.

Only occasionally did I get it wrong and want to confront a harmless person. I remember once, on the way to Danceworks, I was sitting on the Tube when this guy started staring at me, winding me up.

'What you looking at?' I snapped as his eyes bored into me.

He carried on looking at me, not intimidated in the slightest.

'You're the seventh son of the seventh son, aren't you?' he said quietly.

A shiver ran down my spine as I thought of the old bloke in the canteen at Heathrow Airport. What was it with people and this seventh son business?

'Yeah, I am,' I admitted. 'And…?'

'I guessed you might be,' he said, before getting off at the next stop.

I watched as he walked away, my mouth agape, and mulled over what had happened all the way to work. I still hadn't ever looked into my Irish roots – perhaps I should do? How odd was it that total strangers were approaching me about my place in my family. Perhaps there was something in it?

*

If my work life remained colourful, my personal life matched it. For years now I'd had a thing about dating policewomen. It doesn't take Freud to work out what that meant; all kinds of things about power and authority (or fucking authority!). But whatever, if I knew a bird was a copper, I saw it as a challenge to seduce her. Then, in 1997, whilst I was minding the door at a club in East London, a copper called Anthea walked into my life. I can recognise a copper when I see one a mile off. She walked past me, nose in the air, wiggling her bum in her tight trousers, and I couldn't take my eyes off her.

'Hello, hello, hello,' I said. 'Fancy taking down my particulars, do you?'

She stared at me. 'Very original. How did you guess?'

I laughed. Policewomen always have a certain look, bobbed hair and a particular air about them. And I fancied this one rotten.

'He's been on TV, you know, love,' said one of the other bouncers, Lee.

'*Crimewatch*, was it?' she smiled.

I found out her name was Anthea and I couldn't leave her alone. She was prim, proper and posh – the exact opposite of everything I was and so right up my street. By the end of the night, she'd given me her phone number. None of my previous relationships had lasted longer than a few months, but with Anthea things felt different from the start. She didn't mind my door work and I fell in love.

After a few weeks of us seeing each other, she even invited me up to Suffolk to meet her parents.

'I hope you'll like each other,' she said nervously.

I got the impression Anthea's folks were high-flyers like her. She'd been promoted to sergeant young and was on a commissioning board for race relations. But the more I got to know her, the more I began to think, in her own way, she was as screwed up as I was. Her ex had beaten her up and she was always feeling insecure about something or other. But I was serious about her, and happy to go and meet her family.

We arrived on a Friday night for a weekend away, taking a taxi from the train station to the end of a long driveway. Her house was huge, and when her dad opened the door to show me the deer he had shot for our dinner, I was staggered.

This is another world, I thought. Already I worried if I was good enough for the likes of him.

Now I can see that the real attraction we felt for each other was down to our own damage. In her own way, Anthea had a rough ride growing up, with parents who always criticised her, making her feel not good enough as a kid. She'd grown into an adult with as little self-esteem as I had. This was a wake-up call to me. You could have rich parents and still be neglected. Who knew?

Anyway, months into our relationship we decided to book a little weekend away to Cornwall. We were due to leave on the Saturday morning and I was going to do a one-off door shift on the Friday night.

For many years now I had successfully run my two parallel lives alongside each other. But inevitably I couldn't carry on unscathed; some night something was bound to go horribly wrong for me. And when it did, it happened quite spectacularly.

On this Friday night, a warm summer's evening, I was minding the door with another doorman for this place called The Taverna. It had two floors, a wine bar upstairs used by local gangsters and a popular bar downstairs for the other punters. It was a decent place, so we were all monkey-suited and dickie-bowed up, and hopeful for a quiet night as there were only two doing this shift. The night started peacefully enough with a big queue building up but little sign of trouble, until five blokes bowled up to the door, ignoring the roped-off area.

'Hey, we wanna come in,' said one, looking like he owned the gaff.

'Nah, there's a queue there, mate,' I replied.

Then the other doorman stepped in. 'Hey, Jacko, let them in. They'll be my responsibility. They'll be no trouble,' he promised.

I didn't like the look of any of them, but as a professional courtesy I let them go by, even if it was against my better judgement.

Then, just five minutes later, the barmen had pushed their red panic buttons, so I bolted inside. Sure enough, the five idiots were kicking off.

'Who the fuck let these in?' the manager screamed at me as I attempted to calm everyone down.

Turned out the guys had barged straight upstairs into the upper wine bar and had been dropping lit fag butts into the cleavages of the girls below. When asked to leave they'd refused, and now it was my job to get them out.

'Come on, boys. Outside, now,' I said, walking backwards.

I coaxed them out the door like a sheepdog handling sheep. So far, so good.

As we walked outside I glanced up at the CCTV camera, which usually pointed at the door, to check what was being recorded in case it kicked off, but I saw it was pointing at a nearby alleyway. The queue outside had grown even bigger by now, with a big bunch of girls shivering in little dresses and high heels down the side of the building. My instinct was to keep the idiots away from the punters, but I could smell the anticipation for a fight in the air.

To make matters worse, I realised the doorman who'd let them in had disappeared.

The fucking arsehole, I thought. *He probably knows full well what these muppets are capable of.*

I barely had time to react before one of the men – a fat, bald guy – went to headbutt me. Instinctively I threw him an upper cut, smashing into his teeth so he had to spit them on the ground. Then I had all five on me like hyenas, with boots and trainers coming from all directions. Those split seconds slowed as punches came down on me. An egg had already formed on my head and I was covered in blood, not knowing what was mine and what was theirs.

If you don't get out of this, you'll be drinking from a straw for the rest of your life, Paul, I thought as I tried and failed to avoid blows.

Then I heard an echo from one of the old bouncers I'd come across, Ronnie Redruff, who I once worked the door with at Kings in Ilford. Ronnie was a former middle-heavyweight champion and the kind of doorman you'd give a wide berth, with his squashed nose and wrists that were fucked from how many punches he'd thrown over a lifetime. But he also had a heart of gold and was often happy to chat and impart words of wisdom. He worked with Lenny McLean, one of the biggest known gangsters in the area whose life went on to be featured in *Lock, Stock and Two Smoking Barrels*.

One of Ronnie's sayings was this: *'Paul, it's better to be tried by twelve men in this lifetime than carried out by six for the next.'*

With Ronnie's sage advice firmly in my mind, I found the strength to throw another punch into the mouth of the fat bloke. While he wailed on the ground, three of them stood back and I picked up the other one and threw him through a glass door. He ended up shrieking in pain, and I turned to see the other three running off.

Bloodied and bruised, I sat on the ground for a breather. Then I saw blue lights. It didn't take the coppers long to spot me. I was coated in so much red blood it looked like I'd been working all day in a butcher's.

I was used to dealing with the Met from my door work in London when there was trouble, but the Essex police always seemed to go by different rules and they were eager to see me nicked. At first I was confused. After all, I'd been set upon by five blokes. Surely I couldn't have been expected to roll over and be killed? For without a doubt in my mind that's what would have happened.

'Paul Connolly? You need to come with us,' one said.

Down at the Brentwood nick, I was ordered to remove my blood-drenched clothing for forensics and put on a white suit. Then they took photographs of my knuckles, as one of the attacker's teeth was still embedded in my skin. I ached and hurt all over and needed medical attention myself. But they said no doctors were available and, more crucially, neither was a solicitor.

'We need to know what happened, Paul,' said one copper.

I said I'd tell them once I had legal representation. I knew the law and my rights. But they insisted the duty solicitor wasn't available.

'Look, Paul, we're not interested in you. We're interested in the other guys. That's who we want. So just tell us what happened and we'll take it from there.'

By now it was in the early hours and I was exhausted, so I said I'd talk when the solicitor was free the next day. After a fitful night's sleep, I woke up to find Ian and Anthea had been over to drop off some clean clothes for me. I was gutted, full of worry about what they'd both think. Especially Anthea, as I overheard officers ribbing her for being in a relationship with the guy who was now banged up.

I got dressed and was then brought sausage and beans by a female officer wearing a tight blouse smelling of perfume. She sidled up to me, asking if I was ready to talk now. I said no again, but then thought perhaps I should just have quick chat, even without a solicitor present, so I could go home. I was supposed to be on the motorway by now with Anthea for our Cornwall getaway. Maybe we could even make it for one night still?

'Are you sure, Paul? We just need a statement and then you can go,' she repeated.

'Okay then,' I conceded. I had to trust them. They were coppers, after all.

I sat on the hard plastic chair in the interview room and started talking. The police asked what had happened and then quizzed me about the level of force used.

'Did you use excessive force?' one asked.

'I was in fear for my life,' I explained honestly. 'I had to take whatever actions I needed to.'

And that, I thought, was that. So when they disappeared and then returned to charge me with grievous bodily harm, I was completely gobsmacked.

'You what?' I cried. 'But they attacked ME!'

Now I insisted on seeing a solicitor, but it was all too late. The police had a taped interview that they viewed as a confession to the use of excessive force. I was bailed and allowed to go home, but faced a trial by jury the following year on Section 18 (Grievous Bodily Harm with intent) and Section 20 (Grievous Bodily Harm).

I returned home completely devastated. I knew full well I was set to lose everything I'd built up. My career. My friends. Maybe even my house.

How the fuck did this happen? was all I could think.

For so many years I had fought genuine hardship to build a better life for myself. Now I was facing a ten-year stretch for one night's bad luck.

Sitting in my living room, I called Anthea to tell her the news, but she'd already been teased by her colleagues about my arrest. She came over and I was so relieved to see she appeared to be standing by me. She was one of the best things that had happened to me for a long time.

'I don't know what I'd do without you,' I said to her.

Anthea even gave me a set of her house keys, which I took as a sign of her trust and seriousness about me. This felt good, as I knew getting gyp from her colleagues about my charges stressed her out.

'They keep telling me, Paul, you could go down for ten years. As if that's not on my mind already,' she said.

'It won't come to that,' I replied. But deep down I had no idea.

Although we missed our trip to Cornwall, Anthea had booked a holiday to Thailand before we'd met for a week later. I knew I'd miss her, but I was happy she was standing by me despite the problems it caused her professionally. So I kissed her goodbye on the way to the airport and told her to have a good time.

A few days before she came home, I let myself into her flat to arrange a welcome home. I filled the cupboards up with food, made the place spotless and set up a candlelit dinner. I wanted to show her what she meant to me. But the look on her face as she opened the door told me everything I needed to know.

'Alright, Paul,' she said, reluctantly accepting a peck on her cheek.

This wasn't the homecoming I was expecting. We sat down on the sofa, ignoring the meal I'd prepared.

'You've got to leave,' she mumbled. 'I'm sorry but it's over. I can't do this. I've had time to think, and we need to end it.'

I stared at her, looking so tanned and beautiful. How could this happen? But I understood. She was a copper, and I was possibly months away from being a jailbird for a decade. I placed her door key on the dining table and left.

Chapter 18: Day of Reckoning

My trial date was set for eighteen months' time and waiting for it felt like torture. Everything I'd spent so long building up fell apart at a scary speed. Anthea was gone. The phone stopped ringing for celebrity work and I worried about taking on door work. Even going to the gym and exercising didn't take my mind off my bleak future. Things didn't feel like they could get any worse. Famous last words, though, right? A few weeks later one of the gangster associates got in touch.

'Listen, Jacko,' he said. 'I know you've been in a spot of bother, but we need you on the door. I'll pay well and it's just for a night.'

'Nah, I can't, mate…' I began. But he insisted I listen to him and so, not wanting to piss him off, I did so.

'You can have that bulletproof jacket we lent you a while back. It'd be great if you did this one thing for us,' he went on.

In the end I said yes, as he wasn't the sort you messed with.

Little did I know I faced having to work on the same door at The Taverna where I'd been arrested on the GBH charge. And it was with a doorman named Tasty Tommy, whose speciality was stabbing people in the back of the legs and pulling the knife upwards, ripping open all the tendons. Brilliant. I wasn't happy, but when I turned up the doormen all said they'd look after me.

'We'll deal with any hassle if there is any,' they promised. 'We know you need to keep clean.'

No prizes for guessing what happened next. It started off peacefully enough, until two lumps, one big and one small, kicked off at the end of the night by refusing to drink up even after a twenty-minute warning.

'Drink up, boys. Time to go,' I said again, nicely.

'Aw, fuck off, mate,' the big lump sneered at me. So I took their glasses out of their hands.

'Right, the night's over for you two,' I said. 'Time to go.'

I waited for Tasty Tommy to step in, as he usually did, but he was nowhere to be seen and nor was any other bouncer.

Don't say anything, I thought. *Just get them to leave.*

I nodded them to the door and thankfully they started moving, but not without abusing me first.

'Fucking little doorman. Look at the size of you. I've had bigger shits than you!' the fat lump said.

I looked around me, expecting someone, anyone, to take control, but still nobody intervened.

'You're an ugly fucker, ain't you? Seen scum like you before. Need a good kicking, doncha?' said the small lump.

Don't rise to it, I thought. *Stay cool. Do not rise to it.*

But they carried on.

'Fucking scumball.'

'Fucking dickhead.'

'Bet you couldn't punch your way out of anything.'

By now we were outside and I followed them, glancing up at the CCTV camera above.

It was the same club, same road, same camera as last time. I couldn't allow myself to get into a fight. Not again!

They started to walk away. Tasty Tommy overheard them now and he watched me as they continued the abuse.

'Irish lowlife. Fucking pussy!' one shouted.

Something snapped and, knowing the camera was pointing the other way, I finally yelled back.

'Come here and say that to my face, you fat cunt!'

Instantly the big lump turned and ran towards me. But my fists were waiting and with two swift hooks I knocked him and then his mate out cold. Now I was in the shit, especially as my car was parked right opposite the club.

Tasty Tommy knew how much trouble I'd be in if police arrived. 'Just go,' he yelled. 'We'll get someone to drive your car home.'

I fled. Back home, I thought about what a close call it had been. Despite promising myself to stay out of trouble, somehow I'd managed to land right back in it again. I could only hope nobody would follow up on this.

Later on, I heard that the two bullies who'd taunted me were taunted themselves in their local for being knocked out by the 'littlest doorman in the town'.

*

Ian stepped in to try to take my mind off my impending case by inviting me out to San Francisco, where he was working. Thankfully I managed to get permission from the magistrates' court to travel, as I was still on bail. The trip could have been fun, but I couldn't relax for a minute.

One day, while we were standing on the Golden Gate Bridge, Ian suggested we visit Alcatraz.

'You having a fucking joke, mate?' I said. 'Taking a trip around one of the most famous prisons in the world is not really going to be fun for me.'

He apologised, not having realised how I felt. The prospect of going to prison was now very real, and it felt like everything Auntie Coral once told me was coming true. I stood to lose everything and become the lowlife cunt she always told me, day in, day out, I was. I ended up admitting to Ian how I felt.

'They were right all along,' I said to him. 'It's all caught up with me now, hasn't it? I'm going to get found guilty and go to prison, even if it wasn't my fault this time.'

'No, *you* are wrong,' he told me firmly. 'Paul, we've been mates for years now and you're a good, decent man. Yes, you should maybe avoid door work, as it makes you vulnerable to violence. But you don't deserve to go to jail, and hopefully the jury will see this.'

I appreciated his words, but I struggled to feel optimistic. Worse still, my own lawyer struggled too. He said he wanted the taped police interview to be thrown out as inadmissible. If they used this taped 'confession' then yes, there was an eighty per cent chance I was going to go down for ten years. It was terrifying and I hated to admit it, but the words of that evil bitch, Coral, rang truer than any words Ian tried to reassure me with.

By the time the trial date arrived, I was a nervous wreck. I'd tried to get on with my life as best I could, even dating another policewoman called Jo along the way in an attempt to get over Anthea. But nothing I did could shake off the fear I had about going inside. I couldn't see past it. My life felt over. The idea of prison is scary no matter who you are. I recalled a chat I once had with one of the nastiest gangsters I've ever met who did time inside. He admitted to me: 'When that jury returned with their verdict, I was terrified.' And I could imagine feeling the same. The stress got so bad, sleeping became impossible, so Ian suggested I spoke to a counsellor.

'You're fucking joking?' I laughed. 'How the fuck is speaking to some do-gooder stranger gonna help? Is he gonna offer to do my bird for me?'

But Ian persisted and gave me the number of a local guy called Terence. After another week of no sleep, I decided to give him a go. I was that desperate.

Terence was a softly spoken, rather effeminate-looking older geezer with a nice way about him. Instantly I felt relaxed in his company, something I wasn't expecting to happen. He told me about his two chairs: the blue one was for the analytical work and the red one was for being hypnotised. I didn't fancy any of that, control freak that I am, but he persuaded me hypnosis might help.

'We could take you back to your childhood, where things started to go wrong, and see if we can recognise patterns of feelings,' he explained.

I thought it sounded like bullshit, but now I was sitting there I decided I had nothing to lose.

'Go on then, you can try,' I laughed, thinking no way was anyone going to manage to hypnotise me. But after a few minutes of listening to his soft, caring voice I found myself drifting off. Then the next thing I knew I was back at St Leonard's.

The long driveway to the cottages. Holding Mr Gardener's hand. Bill Starling and Auntie Coral's faces looking down at me.

Terence talked me through meeting myself as that eight-year-old arriving at St Leonard's. He got me to describe how that boy felt.

'Scared,' I admitted. 'Really worried. He feels very alone in the world.'

'What do you want to say to that little boy, Paul?' he asked. 'As the adult you are today.'

'I dunno,' I said, feeling myself well up. My little-boy self looked so unhappy, it broke my heart.

'Do you want to tell him anything? Maybe tell him you'll always look after him? That you can take care of that part of yourself now as a thirty-five-year-old man?'

'Yeah,' I said, tears sliding down my face. 'I will look after you, mate. I am here for you.'

By the end of the session I was in bits.

For the very first time in my life, Terence had taught me I could look back at my childhood with a sense of compassion. He told me none of it was my fault and I needed to understand that. I could hear his words, but it was hard to believe what he said, especially after all the years Auntie Coral had told me otherwise.

I continued to see Terence for a good few months, exploring how and why I felt like I did. He suggested I'd built up my sense of self-esteem through fear and violence towards men and having lots of flings with women.

'You were violent at St Leonard's to save yourself, Paul, and this is a learned behaviour you no longer need to survive as an adult,' he explained.

I listened to his theories and it was hard not to agree with them.

'You're a good guy, Paul,' Terence reassured me. 'An inherently decent man. That's why you have good friends and a good job. I can tell from what you've said to me that you're decent, with a heart. There's a conflict with that and the violence, isn't there?'

He gave me so much to think about. I'd begun to consider a whole new perspective on my life.

*

I still, however, faced my biggest fight yet, the one to prove my innocence. Finally, after so many months of waiting, the date of the trial arrived. On the day, I suited and booted myself up, determined to create a good impression on the court and the jury.

Despite being profoundly nervous, in court I listened intently to the evidence given, following proceedings as best I could. At first all the evidence seemed damning – the taped confession, the witness statements from the muppets involved, the sight of me, a doorman, in the dock. A police sergeant even stood and insisted the taped confession was legal and that he was not corrupt, after the judge ruled it wasn't inadmissible.

After a few days I was convinced I'd be in the slammer by the end of the month. But then things started to swing back in my favour. The fat, bald guy took the stand and gave a slightly conflicted account, even using bad language in the dock. He couldn't seem to remember if I'd headbutted him first or kicked him, and when my lawyer questioned him he got annoyed. I could tell by the jury's faces they weren't impressed.

Then, Ray Tame, from one of the clubs I worked in, Palms, took the stand as a character witness. He said in my defence that it was my job as a doorman to protect the innocent people in the queue.

'The priority for doormen is to protect innocent bystanders,' he explained. 'That's what Mr Connolly was doing.'

At that point I noticed jury members scribbling this valid argument in their notes and looking at me sympathetically.

I also had a fair few white-collar types who had become friends and associates through my work as a trainer come and give character statements for me. I imagined the judge was surprised at the circles I hung out in, especially with my accent and background in door work.

Then, to my great surprise, Anthea turned up, day after day. She stood in the stand to give evidence in my favour, vouching for my good character. I was touched by her words and support. She didn't have to do this, especially as our relationship was over.

But the trial was far from over. In spite of these small wins, overall things were not looking good. Any hope I had was dashed yet again when the barrister advised me of alternative pleas in the light of the way things were going. He explained if I admitted to Section 20 (GBH), then I could avoid being convicted of a Section

18 (GBH with intent), a much more serious crime, and I would receive a lesser sentence.

'No,' I said stubbornly. 'It ain't fucking happening. I didn't do anything wrong that night, so I can't bring myself to stand there and say I did, whatever the advice is.'

It was a high-stakes gamble that meant I could go down for a long time. But if I hadn't fought back that night, I remained convinced I'd be dead or at least having soup for breakfast, lunch and dinner.

'Okay, Paul,' said my barrister. 'This is your decision to make.'

The impression I got was that he didn't hold out a huge amount of hope for me. So by the time the summing-up was finished, I was beside myself with fear. I started packing up my house. I'd been advised to get all my affairs in order as if I was found guilty on the day then I'd be whisked straight away for HM's pleasure.

On the day of the verdict, I was completely convinced I was going down. I had my last breakfast at home, handed Ian my door key and told him where everything was.

'Thanks for being there for me, mate,' I said.

'It's not over yet, Paul,' he replied.

'Yeah, whatever,' I said.

On the way to court, I saw a single magpie from the car Ian was driving and the old saying 'One for sorrow, two for joy' sprang into my mind.

'That's it!' I cried. 'That single magpie is proof this will all go tits up.'

We watched as the bird shat all over the windscreen. Ian quickly put the wipers on, smearing it everywhere.

'There you go' he said. 'We've cleared the shit, so it's cancelled out.'

'Why do you always have to be so fucking positive?' I groaned.

Court that day was one of the scariest scenes I've ever walked into, and watching that jury leave the room to deliberate made me feel sick. That nasty gangster had been right. Seeing them return to deliver their verdict was terrifying. They'd only taken an hour to deliberate as well.

'Is this good news?' I whispered to my lawyer.

He remained tight-lipped. If a jury doesn't stay out for long, they tend to think it's a straight, cut-and-dried case. The room started to swim when the foreman stood up and I felt barely able to breathe.

'How do you find the defendant on the charge of GBH? Guilty or not guilty for Section 20?' asked the judge.

'Not guilty.'

I gripped the little shelf in front of me so hard my knuckles turned white. This meant only one thing, surely: I was to be found guilty of the more serious charge. I closed my eyes, feeling as if my whole life was flashing before me.

Me in the home. Me with Liam drinking milk nicked from people's doorsteps. Auntie Coral screaming 'prison fodder'. Me turning my back on my old life. Me boxing. Me in a TV studio talking to famous faces. Me on the pavement covered in blood. Fighting, fighting, always fighting…

'How do you find the defendant on the charge of GBH with intent, guilty or not guilty?'

I squeezed my eyes shut as I heard more words and then opened them, waiting for the coppers to cuff me. Then I heard cheering break out from my friends.

Guilty. Guilty. Guilty.

I opened my eyes. Why the hell was everyone cheering? Then I realised I'd completely misheard what the foreman had said! I'd been found *not* guilty.

'You are free to go, Mr Connolly,' said the judge. He went on to imply what a waste of money the case had been.

Unable to think straight, I did what I've always done when overwhelmed: I ran as fast as I could. Pushing past everyone, I dashed into the corridor, where I collapsed in tears. The tension of the last year was finally released. I wasn't going to prison. I wasn't going to end up where they always said I would. I was free.

'You okay, Paul?' asked Ian, helping me to my feet.

'Think so,' I breathed. 'Let's get out of here.'

I felt as if I had been reborn, been given a second chance. I never, ever wanted to see the inside of another courtroom again. I went home to celebrate, call up old clients, focus on my life and career again. I didn't want to waste a single minute.

*

Shortly after the trial, Anthea got in touch to say she wanted us to give it another go. But she'd broken my heart so badly, there was no way I wanted to go through that again and so I told her it was over. Besides, I was seeing the other copper, Joanne. That didn't work out either and, later on, I heard they'd compared notes about me when they coincidentally ended up on a training course together. Perhaps, I thought, I should give police ladies a wide berth. Instead, I bought a cat for company. I named her Sausage, because when I looked to see if she was a boy or girl, she didn't have one!

No doubt about it, the trial felt like a profound turning point in my life and for the first time in years I longed to get in touch with someone special again. Mary. I hadn't seen Mary now for over twenty years and I was keen to reconnect. Now I didn't have the GBH charge hanging over my head, I was no longer ashamed of my life, and I wanted to let her know I was doing well. Perhaps she'd even be proud of the good bits of my life.

Ian helped out by finding an old letter from her and he wrote to her at the address in the New Forest, asking her to get in touch. We got a reply a few weeks later. Mary had actually moved, but luckily her neighbour hand-delivered the letter to her new address. Mary couldn't have been happier to hear from me. I sent her my phone number and days later her lovely voice was on the end of the line.

'Hearing your voice again is wonderful, Paul,' she said, still sounding just like the Queen. 'I spent a long time trying to work out where you were. Nobody from St Leonard's would tell me.'

'Yeah, they weren't nice there, Mary. But it's all over now,' I reassured her.

We chatted for hours, catching up. Mary had had her own struggles, as she'd broken her back in a riding accident, but luckily she had made a recovery. I told her all about my business and being a personal trainer.

'I'm head of training for David Lloyd gyms in the South East,' I said, allowing myself to feel a little pride. 'After doing well at boxing, I set up my own business.'

Mary went quiet and then told me something quite astonishing.

'You know, Spencer is a head trainer for David Lloyd gyms too, in our area,' she cried.

It was a bizarre coincidence and neither of us could believe it. By the end of our call we'd arranged for me to go and visit her that Christmas.

'You're always welcome in my home,' Mary said.

I was so pleased that her reaction was warm and positive. I hoped it would be the start of a whole fresh new chapter for me. But with all the best will in the world, this wasn't going to be easy.

Chapter 19: The Knock

Despite my dogged determination to change and put my violent past behind me, my resolve was soon put to the test. Although I could focus on my personal training rather than door work, I couldn't stop driving my car and I seemed to attract every tailgating nutter going. Within weeks of vowing to change all my ways, my temper flared again. It was while driving from East London back home that a car came up behind me in the fast lane, the driver flashing his lights and giving me the wanker sign. I found myself gripping my steering wheel, taking deep breaths, determined not to rise to his behaviour. Then I swerved into the slow lane to shake off the dickhead behind.

Don't rise to it, Paul, I told myself. *Just get out of here.*

I thought that would be the end of it, but no, he swerved to tailgate me again, continuing to wind me up. I stopped at traffic lights and so did he. He leapt out of the car, angry at me, so that was it: I snapped and got out too. For a very angry man I'd managed to hold off for so long, but this was too much to bear.

As he swaggered towards me I saw him pulling something from the car I assumed to be a tool. So, not wanting to get hurt first, I punched him fast in the face and he went down. His girlfriend, who had been his audience while he showed off, jumped out, teetering in high heels and screaming as I stood over him.

Only now did I see what was in his hand properly. It was a luminous police jacket.

Oh, fuck, I thought. *I've just hit a copper.*

He staggered to his feet. 'You're in major trouble, mate,' he said, grappling me into a bear hug. 'I need to read you your rights.'

'I ain't going anywhere,' I cried. 'You provoked me!'

He started to grab me, so I headbutted him, ending all conversation. Then I jumped into my car and left.

Back home, I wondered what would happen next. After narrowly avoiding a ten stretch, I could barely believe this now. I eyed the street outside my window. I felt paranoid, and it turned out I was right to feel worried.

The next day, when I drove off to get petrol, I found myself surround by twenty policemen, who arrested me for assaulting a police officer. But when they took me down to Romford Police Station, they thought it was hilarious I'd been involved in an altercation with an Essex copper. Romford, run by Met police, don't like Essex police. They view them as plastic coppers with no proper training. When I explained how I was provoked, they let me off and later I even got a letter of apology from the station.

Two weeks later, I was shocked to see two female coppers ringing my doorbell. I'd kept my head down and wasn't expecting any trouble, so why were they coming to my door now?

Jesus, I thought. *I've not even done anything this time!*

My mind scrabbled for reasons the Old Bill needed to pay me a visit. I'd been a good boy. I'd not done any door work recently. I'd not been in any more road rage trouble. I'd tried to cut links with all the dodgy associates I had. But they seemed determined, so after what seemed like hours of deliberation, I opened the door and let them in.

'What do you want?' I asked. I knew the police wouldn't send women out to arrest me, so my mind was whirring. Had someone died? Had something happened? In many ways it was worse than anything I could have ever imagined.

'Are you Paul Connolly? Born on August twenty-second, 1962? Were you a resident at St Leonard's Children's Home in Hornchurch from 1970 to 1982?' asked one, reading off a notebook.

I sat down at the words 'St Leonard's'.

'Yes to all that. What's going on?' I asked.

I watched the policewomen's mouths moving, but struggled to keep up with what they were saying. Then, slowly, the jigsaw of words came together. There was a big investigation being carried out into child abuse carried out at St Leonard's. The first formal complaint had been made a few years earlier, but it had taken years to gather evidence.

'It may take years for our investigation to be completed, as there are many former residents to interview,' one explained.

'We also have to tell you the news of what happened to the others who lived in your dormitory. Out of eight of the boys you lived with, six are now dead,' said the other policewoman.

Then I heard names I'd not thought of for years, and they came one after the other: Simon, Lawrence, Mark, George, Leeroy, Danny... all dead.

'Dead?' I frowned. I'd heard about Simon and Mark, but not the others.

'I'm afraid someone else died too,' she continued. 'He wasn't in your cottage, but we believe you were close? His name was Liam Carroll...'

Her words trailed off and I stopped listening completely. I opened and closed my mouth like a fish, my heart thudding in my throat.

'Liam?' I managed to breathe. I ran my hand over my forehead as I sat back on the sofa. 'No.'

'I am sorry, Paul,' said the policewoman, genuine sympathy in her eyes. 'He was diagnosed with schizophrenia and ended his life by jumping in front of a train at Elephant and Castle.'

I covered my ears as if to block out the sound. I didn't believe a word of it. Liam, mentally ill? He was one of the strongest people I'd ever met in my life. Some part of me had imagined all the boys from the home were doing okay. Maybe they were married, with two kids and a dog, living okay lives somewhere. I even wondered if they'd done better than me in life. I certainly imagined Liam would have. He was so smart and had such a big heart. If anyone thought I had any charisma, Liam had it tenfold. But in the end, it turned out his past had been too much, even for him.

Just as I was trying to absorb this news, there was another blow that even today cuts me to the bone.

'His brother, Seamus Carroll, has been an integral part of our investigation. He told us Liam had been abused from the age of three in the home,' the copper went on.

If someone had stabbed me straight in the heart, I believe I'd have felt less pain. I covered my face, unable to comprehend this. Liam had never said a word to me. I thought of that angry, violent little boy, and suddenly I could see him clear as day. It had all been a front. He was angry because of what they did to him. I couldn't hear another word they said now, as all the wind had been taken out of me.

'Can we call someone for you?' one of the policewomen offered.

I shook my head, and they said they'd be in touch to arrange times for interviews. They wanted me to make a statement about what had happened to me for the investigation, named Operation Mapperton.

'We need you to tell us everything you remember,' they said. 'We need to do official interviews and write statements to go alongside this case.'

Already so many faces, stories, horrors, all twisting in my mind. I closed my eyes to shut them out.

'Fine, I'll give you a ring,' I promised, feeling sick to my stomach.

Once they'd left, the memories and old feelings came flooding back with such force, I was paralysed on the sofa. Only Michael and I were alive from my cottage, and he was serving a life stretch in prison. It didn't seem real. Then I thought of Starling, Prescott and Davies and God knows how many other paedos who worked there. What about Auntie Coral too? I hoped she'd get sent down for child cruelty at least.

And then I thought of Liam. For the next few hours, it was like I couldn't do anything without seeing him etched behind my eyes. Us on the horses, us nicking milk, throwing lemonade bottles, boxing. Us dreaming of a better life. But he never found one; he decided he'd rather end up under a train. I sat there for hours, just me and Sausage, who nuzzled my face as if she wanted to mop up the tears, so I shooed her away.

Late that night, unable to stop crying, I jumped in the car and drove over to St Leonard's, where I parked outside Liam's old cottage. St Leonard's had closed in 1984 and been turned into luxury flats, although why anyone would wish to pay through the nose to live there was beyond me. The outside of the buildings had barely changed, and as clear as day I could still see Liam looking at me through the hazy window and waving.

'I should have been there for you, Liam,' I sobbed. 'Maybe if I'd stayed in touch, I could have done something? Anything.'

I couldn't believe he'd been labelled as mentally ill. I wondered if that was just the easy way out for the authorities again. Maybe he'd been depressed or felt unable to move on with his life? God knows, I'd struggled with this enough times. I thought how I'd been so desperate to leave all the troubled kids from care behind, so I felt less tainted by it. What had once felt like self-preservation just felt selfish now. Could I have made a difference to Liam? Could I have given him support when he felt suicidal? Guilt coursed through my veins like hot poison. At the end of the day, my old friend might have needed me and I wasn't there for him.

'Liam, I'm fucking sorry, mate,' I said, tears dripping off my chin. 'I'm so fucking sorry.'

I sat for hours, head on the steering wheel, sobbing like a baby.

*

The next few weeks were harrowing. The coppers wanted me to sit down and go through all the facts of what happened. I struggled to sleep or do anything without having flashbacks, but everything felt twisted and muddled. I told them about all the beatings, all the verbal abuse; I tried to think about every single event with clarity. But the more I recalled, the more it hurt. And the more it hurt, it seemed, the less I could recall.

The policewomen were very sympathetic, but they were only really interested in one thing: the sexual abuse.

'But I never got buggered,' I said. 'I can only tell you all about Haydn Davies and Prescott trying it on.'

They noted it all down, but I felt frustrated I couldn't help more. I knew it went on, but it was always in another room. Always just out of sight. Always with the most vulnerable kids who wouldn't say boo to a goose.

'You need to go after Coral too. She made our lives an utter misery,' I insisted. 'She told us every day how worthless and unloved we were, and we believed it too! Can you imagine that being said to little kids? She's wrecked so many lives.'

'Yes, but that was mental abuse and we can't arrest anyone for that,' one copper explained.

'Okay,' I interjected. 'But she was known to have sexually abused kids sitting on their potties! And to have sex with underage boys. She used to shag my own brother, Peter. She even had a kid fathered by one of them, and if that's not sexual abuse, I don't know what is!'

The copper looked at her mate with a worried frown.

'Sorry, Paul. It's really tough to convict a woman for sexual abuse,' she said quietly.

I shrank back in my hard plastic seat, feeling defeated. This wasn't right.

'But what about all my beatings then?' I said.

'Again, we don't have any injury photos,' she began.

I wanted to scream. So if I didn't have proof of any rapes then what did I have?

'So let me get this right,' I said. 'You're not interested in prosecuting those cunts for starvation or neglect of us kids back then?'

The officer looked serious. 'I'm really sorry, but we can't do them for that,' she confirmed.

'But that means people like Auntie Coral will get off scot-free,' I said.

She looked at her hands.

I had blocked out so many of the worst memories, it was a testing time. I got myself a solicitor and we talked through what had happened.

'You're minimising what happened, Paul,' he explained. 'This is a very common occurrence for abuse victims. You say you weren't sexually abused, but the fact of the matter is there were attempts made by Prescott and Davies to abuse you.'

I was also in line for compensation, along with many other victims, although I thought all the money in the world wouldn't make up for what we'd gone through. I tried so hard to think straight, desperate to help Operation Mapperton in any way I could. Memories like seeing Sonia Reynolds nearly being raped by Bill Starling came flooding back, so I told the police all about that, chapter and verse. I started to wonder why I'd not beaten the shit out of all of them before I'd left. Feeling survivor's guilt, I began to hate myself for not doing more to protect the other kids.

What I didn't tell them about was the Snatch Squads, something I deeply regret now. But I didn't withhold that information intentionally. Those horrific rapes were so harrowing; my brain blocked them out for a very long time. Only later on, after the court case, did all that come flooding back, bit by bit. But by then it was too late to use as evidence.

Because I never had counselling during the process of interviewing, I didn't understand that memory-blocking is a major side-effect of extreme trauma suffered by kids. The Snatch Squads happened when I first arrived and continued until I was about eleven, so that was nearly thirty years previously. The intense fear I felt was something I could never keep at the forefront of my mind if I was to try to live a normal life, and so my way of coping with it was to completely block it out. Only with therapy and time did more of it come out, and memories were revived, vivid and horrible. Even today, I have a problem sticking with therapy or even opening up old wounds with my nearest and dearest.

I was told to expect a court date for the Old Bailey after Bill Starling was charged with rape and buggery and indecent assault of eleven victims aged from five to fourteen. Prescott had seven charges and Haydn was charged with twelve counts of rape, buggery and indecent assault. Originally Haydn had thirty-seven counts against him, but this got reduced as evidence fell apart. Historical sex abuse crimes are very difficult to prove, so I could only hope the police were thorough enough. They'd made lots of videos of victims giving statements and conducted hundreds of hours of research.

It felt in many ways like a dream, one I'd never dared to think could come true. Seeing all those abusers in the dock? That lot facing justice at last? Even if they couldn't get the biggest bitch alive, Coral, it was more than I could ever have believed possible.

*

As we waited for the St Leonard's court case, I found myself struggling day to day, as flashbacks and memories flooded back in. I could be sitting in traffic and suddenly have Starling's face spitting in mine. I could be looking in the bedroom mirror and see Liam's face gazing at me, waving goodnight. Or I could be in the bathroom and hear Auntie Coral screaming at me to clean the bath. Worse still, I dreaded going to sleep, where I was haunted by dreams of kids bleeding and crying.

I'd spent most of my life running away from the horror of St Leonard's, and now I had been forced to confront it in police interviews, raking over in detail whatever I could bear to recall. Victims of such abuse need careful handling, otherwise mental health issues they're already likely to suffer from can spin out of control. This was something I know I struggled with, and it's a common problem.

I tried to focus on what I could control in life. My job was a good place to start. But even this wasn't going quite as I'd hoped. I was never able to capitalise on my *Boxerobics* trademark. Another huge company, calling themselves *Boxercise*, came along with enormous investment and took over. Slowly, my *Boxerobics* classes dried up and I became less of a name in the circles where once I was The Next Big Thing. Thankfully, however, my personal training business continued booming and I was booked up well in advance. But like always, it wasn't long before my past life caught up with me yet again.

This time it was Ray from Palms club offering me £1,500 to do one last door on the Millennium New Year's Eve. It proved hard to resist.

'Ah, I'm not sure,' I said at first. I'd made my vow to go straight after my court case. I didn't dare risk fucking it all up again.

'C'mon, Fingers, just this once,' he insisted. 'You owe me for taking the stand at court. It'll be a calm night and I can't find anyone else to work that night. It'll be a nice way to start the New Year, won't it, with extra cash?'

There was no denying this was true. Besides, I'd not done any door work for ages. Surely just once more wouldn't hurt?

'Go on then,' I agreed.

The night began easily enough, but as it wore on and people grew drunker it became rowdier. Then, towards the end of the night, some fat bloke barged past me to get in. I ignored him, putting it down to drunken behaviour, but then he turned and swung at me. He missed and two other bouncers charged in. In the tussle, they held me back protectively, but he suddenly ducked under an arm to clamp his jaws around the flesh on my side. He pulled his head back to rip my flesh like a piece of kebab before spitting it out. I let out a cry as another bouncer kicked him off me. Clutching my side, I turned on the bouncers who had been holding me back.

'You fucking cunts,' I cried. 'Do you know how to do your job?'

The adrenalin pumping, as well as the blood from my side, I ran outside to find the cunt who'd bitten me.

'Fingers! The CCTV is up there,' Ray yelled, but I was long gone.

'I'll find him in the car park,' I yelled back. 'And if anyone tries to stop me, I'll have them as well.'

'You can't, Paul,' he cried back.

'Oh yes I can, Ray. He took a fucking chunk out of me,' I screamed. I was livid and ready to give him a good hiding.

Ray looked on, horrified, as I stormed around the car park for the cunts. When I found one, I could see, out of the corner of my eye, punters with their drinks gathering at the large window overlooking the scene. Ignoring them, I swung a swift left hook at the fella, knocking him out cold. Then I collared the guy who'd taken a chunk out of me. Dragging him to the side by the window, I punched him swiftly in the face around twenty times until his face exploded into a pool of blood. He flipped onto the side of a car, sliding down the glass and leaving a smear of blood.

Glancing up again, I saw my audience at the window were still watching, mouths hanging open now. I wanted to go back for more, but suddenly Ray had me in an armlock.

'For fuck's sake, Fingers! Stop it! You'll kill him. Stop this. Breathe!' he screamed.

I felt uncontrollable as I itched to make sure I finished the job, but Ray held me tight.

'If you think anything of me, Paul, you will stop,' he growled. 'Calm down and breathe. Can you hear the sirens? You need to leave, before they arrive.'

'He fucking spat out a lump of my body, Ray,' I snarled, showing him my blood.

'Remember how you felt when that jury walked back in during your trial?' he cried with gritted teeth. 'Just fucking leave it.'

'Okay,' I said, self-preservation kicking in.

'Right,' he replied. 'I need to get that VHS tape out of the camera and you need to disappear, pronto. Thanks for your help, goodnight and Happy New Year!'

I ran off, away from the car park entrance where I could hear the police and an ambulance arriving. On the way home, I dropped into Ian's and he took me to A&E for a tetanus jab.

'Paul, there is only one way this is heading now if you continue doing door work,' he said. 'Think about where you want things to go.'

He'd never tell me what to do, but he was right. I'd already narrowly avoided a prison sentence and I had completely the wrong temperament for this job. I was being taunted until I snapped, something that would always trigger me. Why was I continuously putting myself in these situations? It made no sense, aside from self-sabotage.

Over the past decade, Ian had been there to calm me down so many times when things could have kicked off. From being in a hotel lobby when I'd clocked a pretty girl and her boyfriend took exception to it, to being on a Virgin Atlantic flight on a boys' holiday when some drunk passengers began to kick off against young families – he'd always been there as a calming influence just when I started to lose my rag.

'You don't need to step in when there's trouble anymore, Paul,' he'd say. 'Sorting things out with your fists isn't necessary. You're above that now.'

For people who haven't experienced my background, my mentality can be hard to understand. Part of me still didn't appreciate what he was saying, as I'd spent my entire life fighting, defending myself or other people. What did it mean not to lash out or raise your fists against the idiots of the world? Once upon a time it was me and Liam against the world, and then it was just me as an adult. Fighting to make my way in life, fighting to overcome an injury, fighting to learn to read, or just feeling the need to fight something or someone. But my friendships have always been deeper than other people's, as I don't have any family to fall back on, and Ian was a man I held in very high regard, so I decided to listen to him.

'You're right,' I said as we left A&E. 'It's a new year. A new bloody millennium, Ian! If I can't turn over a new leaf now, when will I?'

*

After years of interviewing former St Leonard's residents and conducting a long, thorough investigation, the police finally finished with Operation Mapperton. Bill Starling, Haydn Davies and Alan Prescott were all arrested, and the trial began at the Old Bailey in autumn 2001.

It was expected to last three or four weeks, but I didn't go up to watch it. In all honesty, I wanted to avoid all the kids from St Leonard's still. I had enough to deal with keeping my own shit together without meeting all the damaged souls talking about the case before their turn came to take the witness stand. Damaged souls are a big problem when it comes to historical sex abuse cases. It's really easy to dismiss troubled adults who've been abused as kids as 'unreliable witnesses', and it was one trick the defence were relying on. They used psychiatric reports of kids from care who'd grown up to suffer from mental illness as evidence that their testimonies meant nothing. Can you imagine standing in the dock having your evidence picked apart by legal professionals with your former abusers sitting looking at you? The whole system is stacked against abuse survivors.

I just focused on working long hours to take my mind off the case, and waited for the day I'd be called in.

There was one person, however, who had been in touch: Liam's brother, Seamus. He had lived with Liam for most of their time at St Leonard's and he wanted to meet up to talk. So I invited him down to Earl's Court, where I was performing my boxing classes on stage at the Vitality exhibition. Seamus was the reason St Leonard's was being investigated in the first place, and without him insisting the abusers stood trial, none of this would have got so far. He'd hassled police for years, and even when the first investigation failed, and the CPS refused to bring it to court, he continued hassling them until they made Operation Mapperton a priority.

Anyway, I invited him down so we could catch up. We'd never hung out much as kids, but if I couldn't ever see Liam again, he was the next best thing. I arranged for us to have lunch together, between my sessions on stage.

On the day we'd arranged to meet, I was sitting down, having a juice, when this man walked in who vaguely reminded me of Seamus. He looked much older and so tired, and he had a belly on him like he was pregnant. At first I couldn't believe it was the same cheeky Irish lad from St Leonard's. Quickly, I stood up to smile and shake his hand, hiding my shock at his appearance.

'Alright, Paul. Nice to see ya again,' he said, sitting down as if he was in discomfort.

He saw me glance down and patted his stomach. 'Yeah, I know. I have an ulcer. It fucking hurts,' he explained. 'Stress is what they think it is. Years and years of stress.'

He rambled on for several minutes without pausing for breath. He told me how all five of his brothers were put into care because, apparently, their mum committed suicide – something else I never knew.

'Yeah, they told me the truth when I was sixteen,' he said, wincing again and holding his stomach.

'Sorry to hear this, Seamus,' I said, not knowing what else to say.

'You know Liam was buggered from the age of three or four, dontcha?' he said, wiping his eyes.

I nodded. 'Fucking bastards,' I said quietly. 'I had no idea at the time.'

Guilt, which was never far from the surface, flooded back in, making me feel light-headed.

Seamus looked at me, guessing what I was thinking. 'Did you know that?' he said.

'Not before the police told me,' I admitted.

He shook his head. I noticed his hand trembled a little as he clutched his stomach again. Then he told me his abusive house parents had already died so they would never face justice.

'Yeah, Liam hid it well, didn't he?' he agreed. 'Him all over really. The abuse stopped about the time you arrived. I used to have to watch them doing it to him in the staff quarters. They did it to me an' all. I ended up being buggered senseless by that piece of shit, Davies.'

I felt sick and couldn't eat another mouthful. Seamus went on to tell me that one male member of staff would use a syringe filled with God knows what to put kids to sleep so he could rape them.'

'They've got to get these fuckers,' was all I could think to say, clenching my fists. 'They've got to pay for what they did.'

Seamus hobbled off and as I watched him go I felt awful. The experience had clearly fucked up this poor man's life completely.

I went back on stage for my next session wishing that instead of punching the bags I was punching every single bastard house parent from St Leonard's. All I could hope was that the jury would do the right thing. As little trust as I had in authorities, I wasn't let down in my GBH court case and, with such a wealth of evidence, surely it was just a case of sitting tight and waiting. Justice had to be done.

Chapter 20: Lost Cause

Then came another knock at the door. The two police birds were back. I'd got to know these ladies since the trial and as much as I liked the look of them, I couldn't say I was pleased to see them.

'Come in,' I said. The trial was still ongoing but they'd kept me up to speed.

'I am afraid we've got bad news,' one said.

She could have said that again. The trial, expected to last weeks, if not months, was over already. The judge had thrown out the counts against Prescott and Davies because vital video evidence had been 'lost'.

'Lost?' I cried. 'How the fuck did they lose video evidence? Surely it's kept in a vault somewhere safe? I bet if that was me you lot wouldn't have lost evidence against me.'

The officers looked on sympathetically, nodding. I could tell they agreed with every word.

'You can only draw your own conclusions,' they said.

And, boy, fucking did I. Prescott was a former GP, Labour councillor, executive for social services in Tower Hamlets and a fucking magistrate! In fact, at the time of his arrest he was the chief executive of Toynbee Hall, a charity set up to help the poor and needy of the East End of London. If he couldn't pull a few strings, who could? It was like a sick fucking joke that all the authorities were in on, laughing at the very idea of justice for the kids.

As they spoke, my heart sank further. Prescott was only found guilty of four indecent assaults from the 1970s after he confessed to them; six more charges of assault, including buggery, were ordered to lie on file. He was described by his solicitor as a 'pillar of the community' and, sickeningly, his legal counsel even suggested this should work in his favour, not that his actions were therefore a terrible abuse of trust. I was so angry that he'd got off with little more than a slap on the wrist. Several of the charges brought against him were never heard by the court, presumably because of a lack of evidence or because the kids he'd abused had died or were unable to be reliable witnesses. Worse still, because he'd already served fourteen months behind bars, he was allowed to walk free from his two-year prison sentence.

'So he's out already?' I repeated as I looked at the policewomen's faces. They were struggling to know what to say. But they knew full well how I felt.

'This makes a mockery of the justice system, doesn't it?' I spat.

Haydn Davies was also allowed to walk free after his twelve counts of indecent assault and buggery fell apart. Originally, he had thirty-seven counts of abuse against him, but slowly, one by one, they fell by the wayside.

Only Bill Starling was sent down. He got fourteen years for nineteen sexual offences related to eleven victims, nine girls and two boys. There was one offence of buggery, two rapes, one indecency with a child and fifteen indecent assaults. He was acquitted of one count of buggery and two indecent assaults, with a further count of buggery ordered to lie on file. From the moment of his arrest in 1999, he'd denied any wrongdoing and this meant abuse victims had to take the stand against him, re-living their ordeals. One detective on the case said publicly that he believed there were as many as seventy victims of Starling, but even that I believe is the tip of the iceberg. This was a man who spent decades looking after hundreds of kids.

Of course, Auntie Coral got away with not facing anything at all, and so did the rest of them, through lack of evidence or time elapsed.

'The whole thing has been one big fucking farce!' I yelled.

All that evidence bravely given by kids, all those interviews, all that police time, all of those painful memories unearthed, for so little. We kids had not only been let down by the system when we were little, but the system had let us down again as adults.

'The whole thing fucking stinks to high heaven, don't it?' I cried, tears welling in my eyes now.

The policewomen gave me a look that told me they agreed but couldn't say much more. They left me sitting there on my sofa, crying again with the cat; this time with unbearable rage.

*

The next few days were hell. My anger was off the scale, to the point that even my three visits per day to the gym didn't do anything to tire me out. This fury had endless energy. How could Prescott and Davies and Coral be allowed to get on with their lives, walking around freely as if nothing had happened? Sure, Starling was inside, but what justice was this? All I could think about was Liam and all those kids they'd screwed up and destroyed. How could they get away scot-free? I struggled to sleep or eat or do anything without thinking about what to do next. After seeing the state of Seamus and hearing about the mess of the other kids' lives, I felt like the last man standing. The only survivor left who *could* do anything! And the responsibility felt very real.

Then the news about Prescott arrived. Not only had he been free to walk, but – unbelievably – he had been handed a prime role as assistant director of social services in Tower Hamlets *after* he came out of prison. Let me say that again: a *convicted* paedophile, who had served a paltry sentence, was allowed to work in a top job, overseeing huge budgets and making decisions about some of the most vulnerable people in society.

My mind started doing overtime. I've always steered away from conspiracy theories, but I had absolutely no doubt that something was going on. Flashbacks were coming thick and fast, and one idea that formed in my mind wouldn't shift. It seemed like the best solution.

I was going to kill them.

I thought about hurting them, something I was good at. But actually, for real justice, I wanted Prescott, Davies and Coral dead. Starling was in prison, hopefully labelled as a nonce with justice of the prison kind being dished out. But the others? Well, they didn't even deserve to breathe the same air as us.

Quickly I decided: I would track them down, stalk them for a bit and then finish them all off quickly on the same day. Job done. But I needed something for this.

A gun.

*

Within hours of my calling up an old gangster associate, arrangements were made. I had to drive to an industrial estate in East London, where a geezer would hand me what I was looking for through the window of my car. I'd vowed after my GBH trial to distance myself from dodgy dealings, but this couldn't be avoided. I'd worry later about how they'd want me to pay them back.

When the day arrived to pick up my package, it felt almost like Christmas morning. I jumped out of bed and got dressed, feeling like I had a sense of purpose at last. This was the first step to seeking *real* justice, I told myself.

On the drive down there, I thought of Liam the whole way, convinced he'd want this too.

'Don't you worry, boy. Jacko's got this,' I said aloud.

'You mug,' I imagined him laughing. *'You're gonna kill 'em, Jacko! Nice fucking one!'*

I pulled into the industrial estate and parked up in the middle of a desolate patch of land, as described in the phone call, and wound down my window. Minutes later a car pulled up. A darkly dressed man approached me from behind, slipped a brown paper package through the window and left without saying a word. I opened it and pulled out a cold dark-metal Browning gun. I breathed deeply.

This will end it. For those three bastards, and for all of us kids.

I put the weapon into the glove compartment and sped off back to Essex filled with excitement. Next step: hunt the cunts down.

Because I knew Prescott was back working at Tower Hamlets in his top-notch assistant director role, I knew he was going to be easy to find at his office. I had no idea about Davies, but was sure I could work that one out by asking around. That just left Auntie Coral to track down. Days later, my brother, Declan, told me he'd heard she was living on a council estate in Basildon.

How weird, I thought. *So close to me.*

The next day I went down there to stake out her house. A plan was forming in my mind: once I knew where all three were, I would put a bullet in the back of their heads on the same day. Probably do the deed in London first, then drive back to Essex for Coral.

It didn't take me long to find the address Declan had given me. It was on a horrible council estate a few miles away. The house was a depressing-looking two-bedroom brick council house, with peeling paint and badly fitted windows. There was a small driveway covered in dirty tarmac with weeds growing out of the edges. You could smell the scent of despair in the area.

So this is where the bitch ended up, I thought grimly as I walked up the road. It struck me that how for my whole childhood she'd told me *I'd* end up in the gutter, but while I'd bought a nice house in a nice area, she was living in some shit hole.

I walked up the driveway to have a quick look through the filthy net curtains that hung in the front room. Then, just as I peered in, I heard a car pulling up. In a panic, realising it was Coral herself, I leapt down the side alley of the house to hide.

What's she doing? I thought as I listened for the car to stop. I glanced around the side wall to see a little old lady emerge. Auntie Coral had always been well dressed when she worked at St Leonard's, but now her grey hair hung scraggly to her shoulders. She wore a beige coat and was carrying a bag of shopping from Tesco, a store only five minutes' walk away. She looked just like an ordinary old lady you'd pass in the street and never look twice at.

But seeing her made me suddenly sweat with rage. Yes, she might have looked like some old dear, but I knew full well what a nasty piece of work she is.

Go on, do it now, a voice told me. *Fucking kill her and it'll be over. It's what she deserves.*

My hands itched to take action, hit her, stab her up, do something. But strangely my instincts were saying something different.

She's defenceless. She's a little old woman. You can't hurt someone like that.

I shook the feeling from my head as I watched this little grey-haired old lady bustle indoors with her bag of ready meals for one.

You know where she lives, I thought. *Just come back another time.*

Instead, I decided to focus my attention on my next victim, Alan Prescott. So the next day I drove to East London, parked up near Bethnal Green Museum and staked out the Tower Hamlets

Council offices. Watching all the council workers wandering in and out, I felt sick. Did they know a convicted paedophile was one of their bosses? Did they care?

I glanced at my watch. It was twelve p.m.; surely he'd be out for lunch fairly soon? Turned out I didn't need to wait for long, as I soon saw the old bastard emerge from the front entrance onto the street. He looked exactly the same as he'd always done, just greyer and with a fatter face.

He turned to walk briskly down the street, a spring in his step. I hung back, my eyes set on him like a hunter's on his prey. He walked quite far, past several pubs, until I started to wonder where the hell he was off to. Then he turned into The Blind Beggar on Whitechapel Road. Now this pub is infamous, as it's where the Kray Twins murdered a rival gang member.

A real criminal joint, I thought grimly. *How fucking appropriate.*

I walked past and saw Prescott greeting a middle-aged friend with longish hair at the bar. The place was jam-packed, so I knew I could go in and have a look at him more closely.

I wandered past him as he sat down in a booth with his mate. Would I really have to do the deed in the same gaff as the Krays had killed? You couldn't make it up!

After doing a few laps of the pub, I bought an orange juice. Just as I walked past Prescott again, his friend, who was laughing, glanced up and I saw his face properly for the first time.

Fuck me… I thought, almost spilling my drink. *It's Haydn Davies!*

I was absolutely staggered. The pair were still friends and I had managed to find them both on the same day. You *really* couldn't make this up. I saw it as a sign I was doing the right thing, as now I could gun them both down together and save time.

Chuffed, I left my glass at the bar and walked back to my car.

*

Over the next ten days, I made the same journeys, watching all three of them go about their business. Luckily for me, they followed the same routine every day. So now everything was set. I had the gun. I knew my victims' movements. Now all I had to do was pick a day to do it.

Then I mentioned what I wanted to do to Ian. He lived just around the corner from me, so when we weren't out on the pull together we'd often meet for dinner. He was a great cook and loved the company at his bachelor pad as much as I did. He knew how upset the verdict had made me and he struggled to know what to say at times.

'It's so unfair, I know this, Paul. But somehow you've got to live with it, mate,' he'd say. 'Move on and try to turn this negative into a positive.'

'A positive?' I spluttered. 'How's that gonna work with them all walking around free as a bird, while we're all living with nightmares still? You know none of it's fair or right.'

Now I had all my plans in place, I told him of my idea. He looked horrified.

'Mate, you know you can't do this. You need help, Paul,' he said.

'What do you mean? I have it all sorted now, Ian. I know their movements. All that's left is picking a time to do it,' I replied. I still hadn't decided on a date as such, I just assumed I'd keep stalking them until I could take my opportunity.

Ian put down his tea and turned to me. 'Mate, please. Will you go and speak to Terence again at least? I'll even pay for it.'

'Nah, he can't help this time,' I shrugged. 'Don't worry about it. I won't involve you.'

'But, Paul! You'll end up in the nick. This time, for a long time. You'll lose your life as well as ending theirs. There can be no winner in this. Seriously. Think about it. I know you're hurting, but this will end it all.'

In all honesty, I never thought beyond the feeling of knowing they were all dead. I fantasised about the relief of knowing justice had finally been done for all us kids. For Lawrence, Leeroy, Michael, Mark, George, Danny, Simon and, of course, Liam, and all the hundreds of others they'd probably got away with hurting. Beyond that, I didn't actually care what happened to me.

As if reading my mind, Ian looked at me and said, 'Paul, you'll end up in prison just like Auntie Coral predicted.'

I flinched at this, but carried on drinking my tea.

The next day, Ian brought round a copy of the film *Sleepers* and told me to watch it.

'I've checked with Terence and he's available,' he said. 'For me, think about it, Paul.'

A man couldn't ask for a better mate than Ian, so I decided the least I could do was humour him. I made a cup of tea and stuck on *Sleepers*. The characters were played by an all-star cast including Brad Pitt, Robert De Niro, Kevin Bacon and Dustin Hoffman, and the story focused on kids who were abused in Borstal for years. When they got out they sought revenge on their abusers, screwing up their own lives in the process. They ended up dead or in prison by the end of the film, much like Auntie Coral said would happen to me.

I stared at the end credits, lost in thought. The film made a good point. But after a few minutes I shook the moral of the story out of my head. That was a film. Fiction. This was real life.

When I saw Ian later that day, I thanked him.

'There was no happy ending, Paul, and there won't be for you either. Unless you change too, revenge won't mean shit,' he said.

I shrugged. 'Revenge is what I want for all us kids,' I answered.

He begged me again to see Terence. 'Just for one session,' he pleaded. Reluctantly, I agreed.

Back in Terence's office, I sat in the blue chair and told him my idea. 'Look, I know you'll say the same as Ian, but I need to do something.'

Terence looked at me with his usual caring expression. 'Okay, Paul. Maybe you should do it then,' he said. 'Go for it. Kill them. Kill them all. Now, how does that make you feel?'

He frowned and leaned forward. I blew out my cheeks. I wasn't expecting this.

I thought of pulling the trigger and standing over their dead bodies briefly before running away. I thought of Liam's face. Of him being raped. I thought of Prescott glaring down at me in the magistrates' court. Him laughing with Haydn in the pub. Auntie Coral carrying her Tesco bag, then her younger self screaming at me.

'If you were loved, you wouldn't be here, you cunt!'

'It makes me feel relieved,' I admitted. 'Vindicated, if that's the right word? Fucking hell, I don't know. I'm just doing this for the ones who died, okay?'

I twisted in my seat. I had the Browning on me as I hoped to stake them out again, so I'd stuck it down the back of my trousers. Terence started talking again, but I stopped him.

'Hold on, Terence. This is really digging into my back,' I said. Wincing, I pulled out the Browning from behind my waistband and laid it on the table. Looking up, I saw Terence's eyes widen with horror. Trembling, he stood up.

'Erm, okay – stop, Paul!' he cried. 'Now, I should call the police immediately, you know. But because I trust you, I won't. But that cannot stay in my office. Please. Can you take it away right now?' He was backing up towards the window, pointing at the shooter as if was kryptonite, and I couldn't help but laugh.

'Shit, okay, no worries,' I said. 'Sorry, didn't mean to scare the life out of you.'

I picked it up and took it downstairs to the car, where I returned it to the glove compartment. When I came back into the office, Terence looked a bit calmer.

'Now, where were we?' he said, clearing his throat.

We talked some more, exploring the scenarios of what would actually happen if I pulled that trigger, the chain of events that would follow.

'This will end your life too, Paul. You will end up in prison like their predictions, labelled forever as a mass murderer. Everything you have built up and achieved will be destroyed. They destroyed your childhood, and they'll destroy you once again as an adult…'

To my surprise, I couldn't stop tears falling down my face.

'But they were responsible for killing the only person I cared about in my childhood, Liam. And I'm the only one left to do anything about it,' I sobbed. 'He was like a brother to me. And what about the other kids?'

'But your revenge can be positive. You can go on and do great things, for Liam too,' he said softly.

Broken, I sat on the chair and cried. When our time was up, I thanked him and left. Whatever we'd said in that room had been powerful stuff, but still it hadn't changed my mind.

*

I didn't tell Ian or anyone else where I was off to that Wednesday morning, a few days later. I still wanted to stake them out, but today the air felt different and I hadn't ruled out that today was perhaps the day. I parked my car in the usual spot in Bethnal Green and waited outside for Prescott to walk out of his place of work to meet his old paedophile friend in the boozer. They were regular as clockwork, these two. I slid the Browning down the back of my trousers, just under my jacket. Ready.

Bang, bang, I thought. *Then straight in the car and race back to Essex to sort out Coral.*

I looked at my watch. Coral usually went out for her daily trip to Tesco at three p.m., and it was only twelve now. Plenty of time.

I followed them as usual, but unusually the pub was half empty. That caught me off guard. I turned to my left, to a booth with a bird sitting in it. She was staring right at me – weirdly, I thought. There was something odd about her, like she was illuminated in some way. I have to admit, and I know it sounds mental, but she looked almost angelic, like she was glowing.

Must be the light from the window, I thought fleetingly.

Ignoring her, I looked across the bar. Prescott was standing with his back to me, chatting away to Davies without a care in the world. I ordered a pint to try to blend in. Out of the corner of my eye, I could see the woman still eyeballing me.

Jesus, what's her problem? I thought. *Usually, I'm the first to give a lady a nod, but there's a time and a place!*

I sipped my drink and stared at Prescott's greasy head, imagining a bullet in the back of it. Then I put down my drink, still aware of this bird staring, and pulled out my weapon. As I turned, I saw her face again, all soft and full of light. She was staring at me now, with a strange look of compassion.

Don't do it! she was mouthing. *DON'T DO IT.*

I was staggered. How the hell did she know what I was going to do? Her eyes were streaming with tears and her face was lit up, almost ghostly. It was freaking me out.

I spun around, gun raised. Punters noticed and screamed. In a panic, I turned to run for the door.

As I ran past the booth where the crying woman was sitting, I realised it was empty.

'Fuck-fuck-fuck,' I cried like a mantra as I bolted down the pavement. I could hear customers screaming as they streamed from the other pub entrance. I didn't turn to look, but ran like lightning back to the car, then jumped in and drove off.

'You fucking cunt!' I screamed at myself. 'You fucked this up. You FUCKED IT UP!'

My anger boiling, I sobbed all the way back to Essex. Back home, I carried my gun inside, trembling with fury. Pacing the room, I screamed. How could I have got so close, only to bottle it? I'd missed my chance. I'd totally ballsed it.

Tears dripping off my chin, I sat down, breathing heavily. There was only one thing for it now. I wanted out. I'd had enough. I'd failed to do the one thing that would have changed everything. Now those cunts were never going to pay for their crimes. So why did I deserve to be here either?

I took the safety catch off, the hammer off, and shoved the barrel of the gun deep into my mouth. My hand shaking, I pushed it hard onto my soft palate.

Do it. Do it. Do it.

Gagging, I closed my eyes, my finger on the trigger.

Do it, Jacko. End this torture… I thought clearly. I thought of Liam, dead. All those other kids, dead. Why did I have to suffer in this shitty world where paedos can go free? My index finger trembled as I slowly began to squeeze.

'Miaaooow!'

I felt a soft face press up against mine. Sausage, my cat, was suddenly at my side.

'Meeeeeeew,' she cried, purring away, pushing her paws onto my arm.

What the fuck? I thought as I nudged her away, but she reached up and pushed her soft face into my ear.

I started to cry as she twisted her tail around my biceps, which shook from holding the gun. Tears poured down my face as she squashed her face into me, purring loudly, as if mopping up my tears. I pulled the gun from my mouth to look at her, barely able to see, and then I laid on the sofa and sobbed.

I woke about four hours later and sat up, blinking in the dark. Sausage was curled up at my side and the gun was on the carpet. Instinctively, I replaced the safety catch and then put it on the table.

You can't even kill yourself, I thought grimly.

All thanks to the fucking cat. I glanced down at Sausage, whose yellow eyes stared back. Quickly, I scratched her head and took a deep breath.

Something inside told me it was over, as I knew deep down I couldn't kill the cunts. Not now. Seeing Auntie Coral as a defenceless old lady and Prescott and Davies as two old men in a boozer meant I'd struggled to do the deed. The only time I'd been violent was when I had someone threatening me directly. When my life was in danger. But now? I was safe – and bizarrely, I was a threat to them. It takes a special sort to kill someone in cold blood. Sure, if I'd had that gun as a kid I'd have killed them. But I was an adult now. I had choices.

I ruffled the top of Sausage's head once more and headed for the door, gun in hand. Then I drove all the way to the Isle of Dogs. Before I had time to think about my decision, I pulled up by the Thames riverbank and lobbed the gun as hard as I could into the murky waters. As I watched the bubbles rise and the circles expand as it disappeared, I sank to my knees on the riverbank and cried like a baby. Part of me desperately wanted to die, the pain was so overwhelming. But I'd chucked the gun away, so that was one easy way to go gone.

I drove home and around to Ian's to tell him everything. He listened intently, without judgement.

'Good, Paul,' he said at last. 'That's it now. It's over. You've done the right thing, mate. Totally. All you need to do now is turn this into a positive somehow. You could do so much good. Get the message out there about what happened. Write a book even! Concentrate on a good way to get revenge. I know you can do this!'

I half listened to my best mate ramble on, putting his usual positive spin on stuff. It was easy to think this was the end of it, but already I had a gnawing worry I'd made the wrong decision. Even today I feel that way. It would be nice to say this was a happy ending with a neat resolution. But life isn't like that, is it? The abusers still got away with it and those kids are still dead.

Chapter 21: New Roots

For months I felt restless, but I tried to focus on what was good in my life. My career. My friends. My house. I tried to live a normal life, despite everything. I was still head trainer at David Lloyd, and I loved my job and working with people from all kinds of backgrounds. At times I changed lives for the better, and I found it healing to help others. From the outside I was a buff trainer, a charmer who didn't have a care in the world and still dated lots of women. Inside, though, I felt a bit lost.

'I don't make commitments,' I used to say to my dates. 'Marriage and kids aren't for me.'

Once, I met a bird at a club and after we went on a couple of dates she took me back to hers. My mouth fell open as she directed the cab driver to the site of St Leonard's. Turned out she lived in the luxury apartments that my former children's home had been turned into.

Fuck me, I thought as we sped down the familiar driveway.

Weirder still, as she led me by the hand to her flat I realised it was on the site of my old cottage. Even worse, her bedroom was pretty much where my old bed was. Talk about giving me the heebie-jeebies. I was pretty sure if I told her what had gone on in this old building, she'd run away screaming. She lay down and we started kissing, but I couldn't shake off the bad feeling from being there. Within moments, I'd already decided this bird wasn't for me, so I made my excuses and left.

On the way out, I spotted the road names given to the lanes off the driveway. One of them was Prescott Way. I started laughing with black humour.

I wonder what all the posh people who live in those flats would think of their road being named after a fucking paedophile? I thought grimly.

Years later, when the truth emerged about St Leonard's, locals started a campaign to have the road names changed. Too right.

Turned out that St Leonard's still attracted people who weren't that nice as this girl didn't take my rejection lightly. She started stalking me, hanging around outside the gym and my house. She even came to Ian's when I went to his for dinner. We ended up crawling commando-style around his floor as she peered into the windows, asking me to come out. After politely telling her to piss off a few times, I finally confronted her.

'If you don't leave me alone,' I said, 'I'll follow you to your place of work and have a dump on your desk!'

The look on her face told me that had done the trick. I never heard from her again.

I thought I was happy enough dating, shagging, having fun; until someone walked into my gym and changed everything.

Jo was a very pretty brunette who I offered to help with the free weights. Once we got chatting there was no stopping us and I couldn't resist asking her out for a drink. I explained my situation: that I dated loads of women and it was just the way it was.

'Nah, Paul, that's not right,' she said, her lovely smile fading. 'If you go out with me, you only go out with me. Sorry!'

She was about to leave and get changed when I stopped her.

'Alright, no worries. I'll do that then,' I agreed. I knew I couldn't let her slip through my fingers.

So I ditched the other birds and vowed to only go out with Joanne. From the first date I was hooked. Here was a woman who was funny and beautiful, but also tough with it. I knew she'd take no nonsense from me. Jo was just twenty-five and I was forty now, but she was so much more mature. Suddenly it felt like this could go on forever.

We became an item and Jo started spending lots of time over at my place. Quickly she noticed I suffered from OCD, as I was as neurotic as ever about the security in my house.

'What's going on, Paul?' she asked, eyeing the knuckleduster.

I didn't want to go into details, but I sat her down and told her about my upbringing. With tears in her eyes, she couldn't bear to hear any more.

'Life is different now,' she said. 'You're going to be okay with me.'

For the first time in my life I felt accepted by a woman, even if I chose to sleep in the back room after we'd done the deed or woke screaming from a nightmare. One thing she didn't accept, though, was my temper. Although I'd given up door work, I was still regularly triggered by road rage while driving around our area in Essex. Usually I only kicked off enough to make the driver say sorry, but occasionally when I was alone things threatened to get out of hand.

One afternoon, I had Jo in the car with me when someone cut me up when I had right of way. Our car was almost hit and I felt my body going into fight-or-flight mode. The driver pulled over after he saw me shouting and then I got out. He locked his car doors but his window was open, so I grabbed his collar and started dragging him out of the car.

'Say sorry!' I barked in his face.

'Sorry!' he whimpered, and then I let him go.

'Fucking prick,' I muttered, walking back to my car. But one look at Jo's face made me ashamed of myself.

'You idiot, Paul! What are you thinking? You don't treat people like that. That's not me or my life. I can't be around you if you pull some stupid stunt like that,' she sobbed. 'If you ever do something like this again, it's over. Got that?'

I was absolutely mortified and filled with remorse. She was right. I loved her for being so moralistic, and now I was fucking it up by reverting to my violent self. I had to stop now or I'd lose her too.

'I am so sorry, babe,' I cried as she glared at me with a mix of fear and disappointment. 'It will never, ever happen again.' I had to mean it this time.

A year into our relationship, Jo had news for me. She was pregnant. We hadn't planned this, but my face lit up.

'That's amazing,' I said. She was pleased too, and we planned to move in together properly.

'I am not living in your bachelor pad, though,' she said firmly. 'If we live together, we buy a whole new place together.'

I insisted on buying another house on a corner plot, and Jo wanted a place near a good school. Once we found a house that ticked both boxes, we put down a deposit.

Once again, Jo rightly told me I needed to change if I was going to be a good dad.

'You need to stop being a dick,' she said. 'I want you to give up as much of your OCD stuff as you can. No more checking locks a hundred times. And definitely no more losing your rag in the car. Being neurotic and angry is not being a good role model,' she said.

I loved her even more for being honest. So I started to check the windows and doors less, and every time we went out in a car, I'd let it go if anyone did anything stupid to me. I say this like it was easy, but it wasn't. Often, if I let a motorist get the better of me on the road, I'd lie awake thinking about it afterwards, knowing I could have easily taught him a lesson. But I recognised this as ego now, rather than handing out justice.

As Jo's bump grew bigger, I couldn't have been happier, except for one thing. Deep down I feared what kind of parent I'd be when the baby arrived. Would I be abusive like my house parents? Would I turn to violence again? It gnawed away at me, though I never breathed a word of it to Jo.

However, the day my first child was born, in 2004, any fears or worries about how I'd behave disappeared the moment I laid eyes on him. Harley was born blue, with the cord around his neck. As he was whisked away, my protective instinct overwhelmed me.

'Will everything be okay?' I asked the nurse desperately as they placed him in an incubator.

'He'll be absolutely fine,' she assured me. 'You can hold him very soon.'

The moment I picked him up, I experienced a deep love and joy I'd never known existed. Instantly, I knew I could never harm him or allow anyone else to. He was the centre of my world, along with Jo. My family.

We arrived home with our bundle, happier than we'd ever been. I loved every part of helping to look after him, and I was in awe of what a good mother Jo was to our new son.

When he reached two weeks old, I had to push away the thought that it was at this age my own mum dumped me outside with the rubbish. This was unthinkable, and I decided the only way it made any sense was to accept she must have been mentally ill.

I just had to push all of my past life even further back in my mind now and focus on the future with my beautiful son, who was going to have the best of everything.

*

In 2005 I heard the news my dad died and for the first time in my life, with my new found stability, I felt curious about my Irish roots. I never went to his funeral because I never really knew him. But I wanted to see for myself where my parents were originally from. For the first time in my life I felt confident enough that I could handle whatever I found.

So I left Jo and Harley at home and flew with Ian to Connemara, where I visited the little village of Kilkieran where the Connolly family started. My father had been buried there, as some of my siblings who stayed in touch with him carried out his final wishes.

The moment we arrived in the area, I was blown away. It was a coastal town right by the Atlantic, but it wasn't just the wind that struck me. It was the sense of peace and beauty too. Empty beaches stretched for miles and the village was pretty as well as desolate. Strangely, I felt a profound sense of relaxation that I'd never experienced before.

'It's like I know I'm from here,' I admitted to Ian. A very strange feeling for me indeed.

We wandered around the village graveyard looking for Matthew Connolly's headstone for ages, with no luck. Not only were there loads of Connolly names, but they were spelt every way you could imagine too. In the end, I stopped a gravedigger and asked him. After a few minutes scratching his head, he pointed out my father's headstone and I went and crouched down near it.

'*He was a decent sort,*' Mary had said, and her words echoed in my head.

Was he? I never got to know him and now, sitting at his graveside, it struck me I never would either. I started to cry, hot tears dripping down my front endlessly.

'I don't know what's the matter with me,' I cried to Ian. 'Maybe it's what it's taken for me to get here, or it's for what could have been?'

He listened to me patiently and waited until I'd got it out of my system. Then I said goodbye to the dad I never knew and we left.

Afterwards, we continued on our fact-finding mission, visiting the house where my parents had my siblings. We arrived at a small house on a modest council estate, where we were both taken aback to see a huge statue of the Virgin Mary.

'Blimey, religion is everywhere, isn't it?' I said to Ian. We'd already come across numerous statues in other parts and there was a bleeding effigy of Christ across the road. Once again I was struck by what a hypocritical lot the Catholics are. For all the godliness everywhere, they cared little for their unwanted kids, didn't they?

We spotted a couple of middle-aged men outside the house, so we asked them if they'd heard of the Connolly family.

'Oh, for sure,' one nodded. 'I used to play with Matty, I remember now, when I was just four or five.'

I asked him lots of questions about my parents, but he didn't know much.

'I just remember you's all moved off to London and that was that,' he said.

I thanked him and we went on our way. I had been given addresses by a few cousins on my dad's side, so I looked them up next. They were all lovely, and just like Mrs Doyle on *Father Ted*, insisting we eat sandwiches and cakes on each visit. As strange as it was to see so many faces that looked like me, they were strangers too. Many were amazed by my seventh son of the seventh son status, and they took me to their local pubs to introduce me to the locals. Soon I found myself surrounded by people staring at me like I was some miracle.

'Let's try the worm trick,' someone said. I hadn't a clue what they were on about but I went along with it. A guy picked up a load of earthworms and placed them on everyone's hands including mine. He told us all to line up, close our fists gently and then open them again.

'You what?' I laughed. But I did as I was told, and when everyone opened their palms their earthworms wriggled away. When I opened mine, though, my worm stayed still.

'As a seventh son of the seventh son, you'll have healing talents,' someone explained. I nodded, not really believing a word of it but wondering deep down if there might be something in it.

After our visit, I came home pleased I'd been. Not learning anything new about my family didn't matter. I'd seen the place and for the first time in my life felt a sense of belonging, which I wasn't expecting.

Afterwards, several cousins from my biological mother's side got in touch and said how sorry they were for what happened to me, but I shrugged it off. It wasn't their fault. I vowed one day to take my own children over there so they would know their roots too.

Back home, I felt more grateful for my own family than ever. My modest home in Essex was ordinary and middle class, but to me was like a blissful palace compared to where I was as a kid. I woke up every day, and still do, completely grateful to be there and not back at St Leonard's. Whatever the seventh son stuff meant, I had managed to keep it together this far despite everything, and for that I was truly lucky.

With my happy new life in place, I felt even less inclined to keep in touch with my siblings. Sadly, Anne had died in her fifties, but I never made it to her funeral. All the others, except for Matty, had struggled with dysfunctional lives. Not that I blamed them for not being able to turn things around, I just didn't want to be dragged down by them.

Matty came to Harley's christening, but we only met once in a while. Then he asked me something.

'You've never heard Mum's side of the story,' he said. 'Why don't you at least chat to her on the phone?'

The idea seemed crazy, but I decided I had nothing to lose. Taking a deep breath, I rang this woman's number, wondering what she would have to say for herself.

'Mary,' I said, knowing I wasn't ever going to call this woman 'Mum'. 'It's Paul.'

After two seconds of small talk, I told her Matty had asked me to ring.

'Yeah, well, it's true you never did know how hard things were for me. It was all your dad's fault an' all…' she began, and as she went on she barely drew breath between her excuses.

Suddenly, I couldn't hear another word from her. After she'd ditched me as a baby and refused to allow an adoption with a loving family to take place, I realised there was nothing left to hear.

'That's enough!' I interrupted. 'I don't want to listen to you blaming everyone else for your choices. You're just the cunt I came out of, at the end of the day.' And I put the phone down.

I believe this to be true: it doesn't matter who gave birth to you. Your parents don't define your destiny. I don't believe we inherit personality traits, I think we can choose to have them. That phone call gave me all the closure I needed, as I knew that woman could never justify what she'd done.

She died on New Year's Day, 2018, and I didn't go to her funeral. I never knew the woman and certainly I couldn't grieve for her. In many ways I'd spent my whole life grieving for a mother I never had.

*

Following the court case, I spoke out in the press about St Leonard's. I was no longer worried about being associated with the place and I felt so angry we'd lost our chance for justice. I also spoke out about kids in care not being able to read and the struggles I'd had as an adult. As my public profile increased, I started working with more kids from disadvantaged backgrounds as part of my personal training. Then, one day, I got a call from a posh bird called Sue Porto, who worked for a charity, Beanstalk, that helped kids who struggled with illiteracy. I had no idea who she was, but she sounded like she knew what she was on about. I filled her in on my story and she asked me to do a talk at a solicitors' office in London.

'I ain't no public speaker, though,' I said.

'Don't worry, it will only be a small group for lunch,' she assured me. 'We're just keen to hear from adults who have actually been let down by the system and come through the other side,' she assured me.

I told Ian about it, as I wasn't sure what to do.

'Oh, you'll be fine, Paul. Probably just be a few sandwiches in an office somewhere.' He winked. 'Maybe wear something a bit smarter than your usual jeans, though.'

So I turned up on the day with a shirt and jacket on, feeling a bit like I did when I went to court facing my ten stretch, not knowing what to expect. Yes, it was in some office, but it was the plushest place I'd ever set foot in, and when I saw some bird playing a harp and silver service waiters I started to worry. Next, I spied the table cards with names like 'Lord' and 'Lady' and I felt sick. This was more than just a few sandwiches in an office!

I'd barely managed to eat the asparagus and Parma ham starter when it was my turn to stand up and do my talk. I had nothing prepared, so I just spoke honestly about being let down at school. How shit life is if you can't read. How nobody cares about kids in the care system and, finally, how learning to read aged twenty-five was one of the hardest things I've ever done. As soon as I mentioned Liam's name I started blubbing and had to stop. The room erupted into applause, but I dashed back to my seat, not knowing how to handle it.

Afterwards, people told me how great a speech it was, but I thought it'd been rubbish. I'd rambled off the top of my head, unprepared, and allowed my emotions to get the better of me. One geezer who introduced himself as Jake came up to me, though, and gave it to me straight.

'You've got a powerful story. You could tell it much better,' he said. 'Take my card and I'll give you a few pointers.' He told me about himself, and it turned out he was a billionaire who liked to donate to charity every year.

'Thanks for being honest, mate,' I said, pocketing his card. 'Appreciate it.'

Despite this being my first time speaking about myself in front of an audience, I vowed to help Beanstalk where I could and I got invited to all sorts of events. Word spread about me and my story, and even the likes of Esther Rantzen met me to talk about stuff for the NSPCC and Childline.

Just when I thought things couldn't get any more bonkers, an actual lord rang me up and asked me to go and meet him. Lord Francis Listowel was an Irish geezer who was one of the last hereditary peers.

'I think you might be able to help me with my work,' he said.

I had no clue what he was talking about, but I was happy to meet up if he thought it was worthwhile. I just couldn't believe where life had taken me: one moment I was accidentally dropping the C-bomb while I chatted to Esther, the next I was calling a lord a mate of mine, which is what he became.

Weeks later, we had lunch at one of those private members' clubs that was like something out of *Harry Potter*. Over china cups and silver spoons he asked me to help him spread the word about how the care system lets kids down.

'I'd like to see it become a job where people need to be educated to degree level or more in order to work in care, so kids have something to aspire to,' he said.

After telling him all about the likes of Starling, Prescott and Coral, I agreed with that. I'd since found out that Bill Starling had worked as a lorry driver before being a house parent at St Leonard's, and Coral had been a toilet cleaner. The pair of them couldn't have been less suitable for such a job. No background checks were done. And as for Alan Prescott being allowed back into a top job at Tower Hamlets – well, it beggared belief.

Despite our massive difference in backgrounds, I found Lord Listowel easy to chat to and said I'd do whatever he liked in order to bring about change. Kids in care needed someone like him to try to help from the top down.

Months later, I was asked to do another talk, this time at The May Fair Hotel in London for their fundraising event. There was Lord Jeffery Archer who was running the auction, Toby Young as compère and Boris Johnson as the warm-up act, and then there was me, Paul Connolly, keynote speaker!

Fucking hell, I thought on the day. *What am I doing here with the likes of this lot?*

I found myself shaking like a leaf. The words poured out of me, but once again I really messed it up as random stories left my lips, from being left on the bin bags to the horror of St Leonard's and school, from being beaten and hearing kids being raped to finally facing the outside world, almost being locked up for GBH and being unable to read or write. By the time I'd finished, my face was streaming as people started to clap, their own eyes welling up. While Boris Johnson had people laughing, I had them crying, and I just wanted to run back to my table and disappear.

Lord Archer came on next. 'Well, I've done some bird too, so I'll follow Paul into the auction,' he joked.

An incredible £170,000 was raised that night and I was proud to be part of it. The icing on the cake was that Princess Laurentien of Holland was there, a member of the royal family I recalled seeing at the four-day Nijmegen march, back when I was thirteen years old. For the dinner, I found myself sitting at the main table with this lot and she got chatting to me.

'I missed my daughter's birthday to be here today,' she said. 'And hearing you speak and seeing what a great event this is, made it all worthwhile.'

I was so touched. Then I told her all about doing the four-day march with St Leonard's as a kid. She listened to me with great interest and it struck me how things had come full circle. If I'd been told as a kid this would happen, I'd never have believed it. I'd gone from the gutter to being listened to by royalty.

*

Meanwhile, five years after having Harley, Jo became pregnant again. I was over the moon. She gave birth to my second son, Archie, in 2009.

Watching Jo being a mum is like a revelation to me. She's so patient, kind and caring, and she has helped teach me to be a good parent too. They are both strong, happy and healthy boys who are growing up in a household filled with love and affection, a world away from the childhood I had. Sometimes I wonder what would have happened if I'd received the care they do, but I don't dwell on it.

Although life has changed ten times over for me, some things never do. I still suffer from nightmares and OCD, and I still sleep with my trusty knuckleduster by my bed. When Harley was old enough to notice it, he asked what it is.

'It's a paperweight, son,' I explained. 'In case I'm reading in bed and need to hold the page down.'

Only now they're older do they know what it's really for, and they accept Dad needs to be able to protect his family. They don't understand from what, they just need to know I could if I wanted to.

I also sleep downstairs, in case I wake up screaming from one of my bad dreams and scare the kids. Poor Jo has had to get used to all of this over the years and accept it. Thankfully, though, I've found a partner who understands me, unlike so many other adults who grew up in care.

I heard from many of them when they heard I'd been speaking out about St Leonard's in the press. A few of them came forward knowing there was compensation at stake for the crimes committed against them. I was awarded a pittance for living through the hell we survived. But that's what society thinks unwanted children who suffer abuse are worth.

Sometimes I'd get Facebook messages and calls from people from my past because they thought I'd have the answers. But then they'd speak to me and realise I don't have any answers. They have to come from within, and we all have to face our own demons in our own way. One of the messages was most surprising, when I saw it came from Auntie Coral's niece.

'*I hope they rot in prison for what they did to you kids, and I am sorry to hear my auntie worked there and was part of it,*' she wrote. '*You don't have to reply to this message.*'

Perhaps I am cynical, but I never replied because I had no idea how sincere she was. Hard to believe anyone connected to Auntie Coral could be.

*

While my personal training business was going really well, I decided to take a course in Reiki. I'd read about the first Reiki master, Usui Sensei, who had gone off by himself to a mountain to seek enlightenment but on his way back stubbed his toe and then managed to heal it himself. It all sounded unlikely, to say the least, but after chatting to people who'd done the Reiki 1 and 2 courses, I signed up for the first one. Afterwards, I found a new spiritual level to my work as a trainer. I started to sense which muscles needed more attention and I'd focus on them.

A couple of clients were referred to me with scoliosis, the spinal condition that often requires corrective surgery. Using different muscle exercises, I found I managed to help them so that hospital operations weren't necessary. Best of all, I helped kids with the condition successfully too. This gave me a huge boost, and slowly more people came to me for my healing work than my personal training.

One old lady turned up saying she needed help sleeping. She told me all about her abusive husband and a catalogue of sad events in her life, but after a few sessions with me she slept like a baby in her bed.

'Thank you,' she said. 'You have a gift.'

I don't know about that, but I was happy to help her. Still, even at my age, my self-esteem is low and any compliment never stays with me for long. But the satisfaction I gain from my work is massive. I think back now to all that seventh son of the seventh son stuff that I thought was bollocks and wonder if there is something in it. Somehow the prophecy of that guy in Heathrow Airport's canteen, that one day I'd be a healer, came true, something I'd never have believed in a million years as that angry, volatile nineteen-year-old.

Then, in 2014, something even more mental happened: I was asked to do a speech in the House of Lords by Lord Listowel.

'Er, I ain't too sure about that,' I said to him. But he assured me I'd be fine.

I got back in touch with Jake the billionaire, to ask for help and tips on public speaking. He even came to watch my speech as well.

'Here, get this down your neck,' he said, handing me a scotch on the day. 'You're going to be great this time.'

Ian and Jo also came to watch me do my talk. I don't mind admitting I was shitting myself beforehand. I missed my cue to go on and had to be introduced about four times before I realised it was me, I was that nervous.

Standing there, looking around that infamous room, a place no boy from St Leonard's ever thought he'd end up in, I struggled to get going. But once I did, there was no stopping me. This time I spoke eloquently and from the heart, not missing out a single thing about the impact the care system has on young lives and how as a society we are letting the most vulnerable people down.

At the end of it everyone rose to clap, with lords and ladies brushing the corners of their eyes. I looked over and Jo's face was beaming with pride as she mouthed: 'I love you'.

Afterwards, Jake came up to me and patted me on the back. 'Congratulations, Paul. You're definitely a speaker now.'

The most recent charity I've been honoured to be involved with supporting is called Kids Inspire. It's a local, grass-roots charity based in Essex that takes on the worst cases of child neglect that the authorities struggle with. They've helped kids live through terrible situations, like saving three- and five-year-old sisters from sleeping under a car while their mum used the home as a brothel and a child who watched his dad stab his mother to death. Today, four million kids are being brought up in poverty, and in the current climate of austerity this will only get worse. Understandably, Kids Inspire is a charity close to my heart and I hope to be involved with raising funds and its profile wherever I can.

*

Despite my own personal happiness, the hideous legacy of St Leonard's goes on and on. The knowledge that the abusers are still out there, walking around living normal lives, hurts not only me but, I am sure, all the kids who survived in their 'care'. Bill Starling has done his time and is out of prison; Alan Prescott was allowed to retire from his post at Tower Hamlets like a normal, law-abiding person; and for all I know a cashier could be serving Auntie Coral in her local Tesco as I write this. And in all honesty, the thought still sickens me. Ian was right that I had to let it go in order to live my life, but on my dark days I struggle with that decision. Just like I struggle with not being there for Liam and with not allowing violence to overpower me day to day.

Thankfully, though, all I need to do to stop myself feeling road rage is look in the rear-view mirror of my car to see the kids on the back seat. Not only would road rage endanger them, but I'd be teaching them that violence is the answer – which it never is. Yet, still, the knuckleduster I sleep with will need to be prised from my cold, dead body when I die.

The physical scars that cover my body tell their own stories, from the cigarette that Starling stubbed out on my chest, to my head being smashed in the bathroom, to being bitten outside the club as a doorman. I am not proud of them, but like my tattoos they show who I am, where I'm from, what I've survived. But with abuse, it's not just the physical scars that linger; it's the mental ones too. Despite all of the love and support from my family, friends and even the clients I help, I struggle every single day to accept where I am and what I have achieved. It's hard to believe that, unlike my birth parents who gave me away, these good people around me are here to stay. But, at the same time, I am so grateful for the love around me. It feels like a second chance at life, which is what so many other kids from the home never had.

Somehow I've managed to let my story be heard in a way I never imagined possible as a kid. Nobody would have listened or cared back then, but they do today, and for that I am very grateful, especially to you, the reader, for finishing this book.

*

So, this is my account, warts and all, even if sadly there is no perfect ending. The horror of the St Leonard's story is still unfolding as more crimes are investigated and more people come forward, even thirty years later. I can only hope that those six out of the eight in my dormitory who died and my best mate, Liam, found some peace. They deserve that at least, because justice will never truly be done.

Epilogue : Mary

"I first met Paul when he was a matter of weeks old and had just arrived at St Vincent's. I was eighteen years old and training to be a nursery nurse, and this was my first placement. In those days, lots of babies were abandoned as women were unable to have abortions. Of course, we were not supposed to get too attached to our charges, but it was impossible not to love this baby boy.

Paul was my first ever love.

He was one of the few who had no home to go to and I was desperate to take him to mine. So from when he was ten months old, I'd whisk him off for the weekend to my mother's house in Ringwood. I wanted to adopt him, but it was impossible for a single woman to do this in those days. Besides, his father used to visit him, although he has no memory of this. He was a sweet man, a bricklayer for Wimpey Homes. He used to work night shifts, then come and visit Paul and his siblings at the weekends.

When Paul was a toddler, I left St Vincent's, but I came to visit as much as possible. I still had him home for weekends, especially when I got married to Adrian. I wanted to show Paul a normal home and make him feel special.

Even after I had my son, Spencer, in 1968, I never forgot Paul.

For several years he still came down every summer and for the odd weekend during his time at St Leonard's. A few times I picked him up from Waterloo Station, where Bill Starling dropped him off. I never trusted that man. Once he handed me a plastic bag full of old boys' underpants.

'Paul wets the bed still,' he said.

I took them from him and replied, 'Well, he never wets the bed when he stays at my house.'

The few times I met staff from St Leonard's I did not like them, but I could never, ever, have imagined just how bad things really were. I would ask Paul if he was okay and happy, but he wouldn't ever talk about it. He was always happy at our house and I accepted that.

Within a few years of being at St Leonard's, Paul stopped visiting us. I thought about him all the time, and when he didn't reply to my letters I started to ring the home on Sunday evenings, hoping to catch him. They always told me he was out or not around. I began to worry even more and started to ring Tower Hamlets Social Services.

'I want to know about a little boy called Paul Connolly,' I said to whoever answered the phone. And each time I gave his details they always drew a blank or said they'd get back to me and never did. They wouldn't even confirm if he was at St Leonard's any longer!

Looking back, I wish I had got on a train and turned up at the door. But in those days you trusted the authorities, and I had a busy life with a family of my own too. I knew Paul was in Tower Hamlets' care, so I had to assume he was being looked after. I continued to write letters just in case, but never heard anything.

It wasn't until years later, when he got in touch with me, that I knew he was alright, and I was beside myself with relief. He was alive and he was okay. He came down that Christmas, in 1998, to see us all and we had a wonderful reunion.

Paul was always a character and I was so pleased to see him grow into the man he has become. Of course, it was very painful to hear what really went on at St Leonard's. I wish I could have gone back and done more to find Paul and find out what was going on.

Today, I am very happy he is part of our lives again. Paul was always a delightful, special little boy and I am proud of the man he is today. I told him often he was special, because he was and he still is."

-

Printed in Great Britain
by Amazon